Praise for *The P*

"The book opens up fresh possibilities of thinking and being, and serves as a window into the soul of a new century Adventism. While disturbing to every form of *status quo,* the book is full of hope and promise. I am thrilled that this book is coming to us at this time."—Raj Attiken, DMin, president, Ohio Conference of Seventh-day Adventists

"Charles Scriven's *The Promise of Peace* will give hope to a new generation of Adventists who desperately long to re-appropriate their faith and traditions in a way that gives meaning to their lives and helps them shape a more peaceful and just world. I will be using this book with all my new members."—Ryan Bell, pastor, Hollywood Adventist Church

"Scriven is a son of the soil and that soil is the Adventist faith community. All of his thought roads lead to his 'beloved community.' In spite of its warts and blemishes, he chooses to identify and suffer with this peacemaking remnant."—Charles Bradford, former president, North American Division of the General Conference of Seventh-day Adventists

"Scriven has given young North American Adventists something to celebrate—a description of our church's heritage and identity, which inspires hope in spite of our frequent failures to live up to our ideals. Reading *The Promise of Peace* made me proud of my Adventist heritage." —Lisa Clark Diller, professor of history, Southern Adventist University

"Scriven makes a passionate appeal for Adventists to be faithful to their high destiny. I am especially moved by chapter 5, which challenges the church to recover its peacemaking roots in a world torn by war." —Roger Dudley, professor, Andrews University

"Scriven, ever honest about life's hurts and horrors, explores the Adventist faith as the practice of hope. As one who takes seriously being and becoming Adventist, I am a better one for having read this book. I look forward to the classroom conversations it will generate!"—Kendra Haloviak, assistant professor of New Testament studies, La Sierra University

"Scriven, writing with the passion of an evangelist, seeks to invigorate a tradition in need of making itself relevant to the here and now. I love and cherish this book. I will make sure that my kids read it."—Edwin I. Hernandez, PhD, Foundations research director, DeVos Family Foundations, and research fellow, Center for the Study of Latino Religion, University of Notre Dame

"Is Adventism defined simply by its doctrines? Charles Scriven offers a fresh and insightful approach: as important as specific doctrines and behaviors may be, they find their basis in the peacemaking mission of God and His people in the world."—Donn W. Leatherman, professor of religion, Southern Adventist University

"Don't get this book if you're afraid to have your faith re-focused, re-energized, perhaps even revolutionized. Or if you're hesitant to spark a lively, well-informed discussion in your class or study group about the meaning of historic Adventism for contemporary times."—Douglas Morgan, professor of history and political studies, Columbia Union College; director, Adventist Peace Fellowship

"This book expresses hope for a radically new—yet historic—way of being Adventist and doing the work of God as a people of *shalom,* which, I believe, lies at the heart of Adventism's apocalyptic dream."—Julius Nam, associate professor of religion, Loma Linda University

The Promise of Peace

Also by Charles Scriven

The Transformation of Culture: Christian Social Ethics
After H. Richard Niebuhr

The Demons Have Had It: A Theological ABC

How to Believe When You Hurt

DARE TO *LIVE* THE ADVENT HOPE

The Promise of *peace*

CHARLES SCRIVEN

Pacific Press® Publishing Association
Nampa, Idaho
Oshawa, Ontario, Canada
www.pacificpress.com

Cover design by Gerald Lee Monks
Inside design by Aaron Troia

Scripture texts not otherwise credited are from the New Revised Standard Version of the
Bible, copyright © 1989 by the Division of Christian Education of the National Council of the Churches of Christ in the USA. Used by permission. All rights reserved.

You can obtain additional copies of this book by calling toll-free 1-800-765-6955 or by
visiting www.adventistbookcenter.com.

Library of Congress Cataloging-in-Publication Data

Scriven, Charles.
  The promise of peace : dare to live the Advent hope / Charles
Scriven.
      p. cm.
  ISBN 13: 978-0-8163-2350-0 (pbk.)
  ISBN 10: 0-8163-2350-X (pbk.)
  1. Adventists—Doctrines. I. Title.
  BX6121.S37 2009
  230'.67—dc22

                                                              2009009538

09 10 11 12 13 • 5 4 3 2 1

Acknowledgments and Dedication

What you will read here are notes on a long conversation.

My seminary teachers at Andrews University challenged and inspired me, especially Roy Branson. So did my teachers at the Graduate Theological Union in Berkeley, especially James Wm. McClendon Jr. My colleagues at Walla Walla University kept the long conversation going, as did my colleagues at the Sligo church, near Washington, D.C., and at Columbia Union College just next door.

For the past nine years, I've worked at Kettering College of Medical Arts, where, as members of the Theological Club know, the conversation is still rich, and where leaders of the parent Kettering Health Network provide a congenial atmosphere for what I like to call the ministry of imagination.

Besides these teachers and friends, there are the books I've read, so many of them like the morning light that scatters darkness. As I hope someone may be grateful for what I've written here, I am grateful for what the authors of these books have bequeathed to me. The endnotes do not begin to account for my entire debt to them.

Several people took the trouble to read chapter drafts along the way, including Raj Attiken, Roy Branson, Lisa Diller, Bonnie Dwyer, Kendra Haloviak, James Londis, Charles Sandefur, Graeme Sharrock, and Daryll Ward. I wish to single out Doug Morgan in particular, who, by way of both his scholarship and his passion for peace, gave invaluable guidance and support.

Bert Haloviak deserves thanks for helping me with details of Adventist history. For their patience and attention, I thank members of the Adventist Society for Religious Studies, who heard drafts of many of the book's chapters at the annual meeting we all love to attend. I also wish to thank Arthur Patrick, who arranged for me to speak on the book's themes at Avondale College in Australia, where my working title (up to that point) began to change into the one you see now. I also owe much to my editors at Pacific Press—to Tim Lale (now at Southern Adventist University), who took a highly encouraging interest in my book proposal, and to David Jarnes, who did all the work on the manuscript. I also thank Karen Pearson.

When, in 2004, I asked Rebekah Wang to read chapter drafts for me, she suspected right away that my request was partly disingenuous. Not long afterward, she became my wife and best friend. Again and again as my work continued, Becky reminded me to shun pomposity in my writing and easy optimism in my theology. Her gift for seeing into the human heart and her awareness of how much we *need* the Second Coming are singular embodiments of grace. As for her habit of pushing me, sometimes severely, toward the finish line, let me say only that without her, I might *still* be fretting over endnotes or looking for another synonym.

All three of my children make an appearance in these pages. Jonathan, Christina, and Jeremy are themselves part of the long conversation. To them, and to Marianne, their mother, I owe much of the joy I have known, and also much of the insight. In its way, the whole book is a father's letter—a record of what he hopes his family will remember about his passions, about why he walks (and all too often stumbles) along the path the risen Christ has set before us.

I return now to James Wm. McClendon Jr. He spoke and wrote from the Radical Reformation point of view. And he gave me the greatest intellectual gift of my life: the knowledge that the Radical Reformers—who broke with Luther, Calvin, and Zwingli precisely by emphasizing how loyalty to Christ transcends every other loyalty—belong to *our* heritage. He taught me that Adventism *is* a Radical Reformation movement.

Jim McClendon died in late October 2000, shortly after seeing a finished copy of volume 3 of his *Systematic Theology*. His legacy, apparent in both the outline and substance of these pages, is challenging; his words both beautiful and deep. I dedicate *The Promise of Peace* to his memory.

This great teacher helped me explore my heritage with new eyes, and come, as T. S. Eliot would say, to "know the place for the first time." The mistakes and shortsightedness in what follows will remind us, however, that if we ever cease from our exploration, we will have stopped too soon.

Contents

" 'I will bless you . . . so that you will be a blessing.' "
—Genesis 12:2

"I will make with them a covenant of peace."
—Ezekiel 34:25

"Lo, your king comes to you . . .
riding on . . . the foal of a donkey. . . .
And he shall command peace to the nations."
—Zechariah 9:9, 10

" 'Blessed are the peacemakers.' "
—Matthew 5:9

"Fasten the belt of truth around your waist,
and put on the breastplate of righteousness.
As shoes for your feet put on whatever will make
you ready to proclaim the gospel of peace."
—Ephesians 6:14, 15

"Grace to you and peace from . . . Jesus Christ,
the faithful witness, the firstborn of the dead,
and the ruler of the kings of the earth."
—Revelation 1:4, 5

"God works out His purpose through a
'remnant,' a minority ready to think and act
ahead of the community as a whole, and so keep
alive the vision of God's redemptive way."
—G. H. C. MacGregor

1

Dreams and Disappointments

It's human to dream dreams. Your heart tells you so. Look inside and you find needs and longings familiar to everyone. You want to be free, not hounded or hemmed in. You fear loneliness, and you yearn for love—someone to share your life; friends and family to forgive you, spur you on, give you laughter and serenity. You see yourself in a satisfying job, a pleasing neighborhood, a peaceful world. You look for joy and beauty—a sunset or song, a weekend away, a dinner or performance to remember. And all the while, you hope to taste adventure, find a mission, and make a difference.

But even though you want to flourish, disappointments happen. You fall short of your goals or lapse into boredom. Your family, company, or neighborhood becomes imperiled. You see those you love pulling away, losing spirit, falling sick. You find tragedy and terror, pitiless as thugs, stalking the planet. Sometimes, as the song says, you feel "like a jigsaw puzzle with a couple of pieces gone."[1]

Or worse.

We live, all of us, in the space between our dreams and disappointments. Whoever you are, life takes turns you can't control. Sometimes you soar, and sometimes you don't; one minute you're hopeful and confident, another you're not. All this is part of every effort to live well, every quest to reach a goal.

Just here is where the promise of peace—the theme of this book—comes in. In the space between our dreams and disappointments, we have needs and wants, so promises matter. And no promise could be better than one that assures a day when high dreams surmount obstacles, when the best of human hopes come true and everyone can flourish. Just such a promise—the Great Promise, you might say—is what makes Adventists *Adventist*. According to the Bible, God has promised to bless humanity and to conquer death and renew all things. Finally, in other words, peace will prevail. Finally, a single "pulse of harmony and gladness" will beat "through the vast creation."[2]

The pages that follow are about being and becoming Adventist—being and becoming someone who sees all of life in the light of the Great Promise and makes that promise the key to both attitude and conduct. The promise of peace is about how to become more fully alive precisely in the space where dreams meet disappointment. I am going to show you how the assurance of final blessing enables us all, despite our difficulties, to live in the here and now with confidence and passion.

Because we are human, with the ability to watch ourselves and to size up what is going on, life is always an issue for us—we're always looking for something better. So exploring makes sense. And the point of exploring Adventist life is to find a better way of being human, a way that will help us, in both sunshine and shadow, to journey on and to stand tall along the way.

The View From Inside

No one discusses a topic from a neutral place. We belong, each of us, to families and larger communities, and the stories of our lives shape how we see and think. So the perspective I offer here reflects my life story—where I grew up, people I was close to, books I've read, billboards I've seen, and television I've watched. In particular, my perspective reflects experience *inside* of Adventism. I was baptized at twelve, and although I have struggled with my faith and read and listened to many people who are unsympathetic to it, I have never left it behind.

I've never wanted to. The great moral heroes—the prophets of their time—take a path from the common places to uncommon ones. They stand apart. They act ahead of others. In short, they dream things that never were and say, "Why not?" And that is what Adventism—at its best—is about. It's about the Great Promise, and about the journey, however eccentric, to the day when songs of peace and gladness resound from earth to heaven.

In making that journey, you want to *live* your faith, not only profess it; and I have tried to do so. But as my experience has widened, I have met challenges to my faith. Some were my own realizations of Adventism's shortfalls: its lack now and then of truthfulness; its readiness all too often to restrain imagination. Some challenges were questions, or even attacks, from people who disagree with Adventism, or who disagree with the Christian faith in general. Still others were devastating events, the kind that make it hard for anyone to trust God's goodness. All these challenges now color how I understand my commitment, but that commitment— that life within the church—endures.

It goes without saying that the church is no easy place where every-thing is effortless. But it's still, as I will say later, the "beloved commu-nity." It's still a place where, as in a family, you can live and learn with others who care about you. And it's still a place where hope thrives, lively as flame. You will find stale sanctimony inside the church, and raw wounds inflicted by the saints themselves. But you will also find the story of Jesus, and you will find people emboldened by that story to live their best and deepest dreams, and to care for you and others in ways that leave you grateful, or even flabbergasted.

Yes, but now a question: among all the religions and all the varieties of Christian religion, why Adventism in particular? I have already sug-gested that I am thankful for the way of life I lead. I want it to be a pos-sibility for others. But how, in an age of postmodern doubt, can I think to make a case for something this specific? When it's hard enough to give convincing reasons for Christianity in general, why stand up for one small family within the larger one?

In major part, that is the subject of this entire book. But to get at the gist of the matter, let me point to the Adventist beginnings we will consider in more detail in the next chapter. Adventism, or the vision and way of life of the Seventh-day Adventist Church, began in the northeastern United States at about the midpoint of the nineteenth century. That was when a small group of people, stung by unbearable disappointment, found, by God's grace, a way to reaffirm their hope.

They had thought that 1844 would be the year of the Second Coming, the year of Christ's glorious return as Victor over evil. They were wrong. Still, these pioneer Adventists began anew to embrace the Great Promise, and to do so with increasing attention to God's creation and God's concern for fullness of life on earth. In 1845, they began to celebrate the same seventh-day Sabbath that Jesus celebrated. It was a weekly memorial, this Sabbath experience, of God's making the earth and also of His liberating Israel from slavery, and this experience gave the first Adventists—when they were at their best—the same passion for wholeness that Jesus had.

A Life Together

When *they* were at their best. Like the believers who sprang into existence following the resurrection of Christ, the first Adventists forged a life *together*. They were not loners but brothers and sisters. They spent their days, and especially their Sabbaths, in the company of one another.

Soon, the first Adventists began to see themselves as a people called to be "the remnant." This biblical metaphor, as much as any other, came to define their sense of special mission. It suggested, as we will see in chapter 5, a community that is both small and courageous—a community eager to follow Jesus against the currents of fashion and convention. The metaphor would become a kind of signature—one more identifying mark of who they were. In time, it would evoke controversy inside the church, but it would live on in Adventist consciousness. It would continue to focus attention on the challenge of true Christian faithfulness and authenticity, as well as on the sense of special mission.

The enduring gift of the Adventist pioneers means that Adventists today look forward to the second coming of Christ. It means, too, that we interpret our hope through the joy and promise of a Sabbath observed on the seventh day, as it was in the beginning. It also means that we see the world, and our lives within it, through a signature metaphor that puts Jesus—His faith, His *story*—at the heart of the Christian experience.

All of this leaves Adventists out of sync with business as usual. All of this sharpens the sense that God has called us to take up an alternative way of life—called us to be the vanguard of a new humanity, a people who, in upholding Christ, keep hope alive and shed a light on the path to peace.

The perspective you acquire when you are Adventist helps meet the challenge of living between your dreams and disappointments. It enables anyone who embraces it to make the journey of life on a bridge of hope, not a bog of pessimism. That is why I dare to recommend—dare to make a case for—this way of life.

Such hope as Jesus had is the key, we will see, to being fully human and fully alive—the key to living our best and deepest dreams with con-fidence and courage. To some, this hope will seem too good to be true. Others will say it is too hard to be good. But no one can make this hope a matter of indifference. You can't brush it off as you would a pitchman at the carnival, not when you occupy the space between your dreams and disappointments. That space is where people deal every day with lacer-ated hearts. And the right hope, after all, is just what damaged hearts require.

The first Seventh-day Adventists, like the earliest Christians, were completely taken with the sense that the risen Christ would make a mag-nificent end to the sway of evil. He would return in triumph, and a new heaven and new earth would take hold. Through and through, these Ad-ventists were a people of hope. In a moment, I will turn to a fuller ac-count of their story, from the 1840s to the present day, meaning to show how their hope matured along with their knowledge and understanding. Then I will tell the larger story of the Bible, with particular focus on Jesus and His first followers, and give brief attention at the end to how Chris-tianity developed down the centuries after the Bible.

These two stories—of what happened in Adventism and of what lay behind it—make up the overall story that defines Adventist identity and gives shape to Adventist life. In what follows, each story takes a chapter to tell. Each is a step toward understanding how someone lives, or must live, in order to be authentically Adventist. Chapters 4 and 5 reflect further on this theme and together lay out an Adventist moral vision, and chapter 5 explores in particular the peacemaking mission that springs up from the church's signature metaphor.

Once we have considered Adventist *life,* the book will turn to Adventist *teaching,* and then to Adventist *witness.* In the second main section, I look at certain core beliefs or convictions and ask what they mean and why they matter. What is the Second Coming about? How does the idea that God is our Creator make a difference? Why is Jesus so important? What's the point of belonging to the church?

The section on the final theme, witness, explores how authentic Adventist life takes its place in the wider world. How, if you are Adventist, do you interact with people who are different—even radically different—from you? What does the gospel commission—Christ's call for us to make new disciples—mean now, when the limits on human knowing and the havoc wrought by arrogance are both so evident? Finally, how can ordinary Christians with ordinary vocations make a truly constructive difference in the world?

Wherever You Start, You're in the Middle

Concerning efforts to explain Christian teaching, Karl Barth, the great theologian, remarked, "We can only repeat ourselves."[3] I note these words because they are a reminder of our limitation and a summons to humility. In at least two ways, everything I say here will involve repetition. The key is seeing that in the exposition of faith, there is nowhere to begin but in the middle. If you are a sailor, you may start your voyage from somewhere, but you won't start from scratch—without ships or shipbuilding, without the lore of the sea, without the social systems that provide cargoes and markets and destinations. And if you bear spoken or written witness to your Christian faith, it's the same. You can't start from scratch. You're already *inside* the Christian story—*inside* God's love, and *inside* the social systems that make witness to God's love possible. You have benefited already from churches, schools, families, and other circles of Christian love in which words and deeds keep the gospel story alive.

This means, of course, that in what follows, I will be repeating what I have learned from others. That is the first kind of repetition you will see. I am attempting a fresh perspective, but it's a perspective on a way of life that was handed on to me. In witness, as in the whole of Christian existence, you live inside a great gift, with every good thing an occasion to give thanks. Paul's rhetorical question to the believers in Corinth says it perfectly: "What do you have that you did not receive?"[4]

In bearing a verbal witness, repetition happens in another way. As soon as you say more than a little, you come back to things you have said before. Again, this is about being in the *middle* of things—but now I mean being in the middle not just of the long Christian heritage but also of what you yourself are trying to say. Wherever you start, you're in the middle.

This book, for example, starts with the Christian *life*. That part of what I will be talking about in the book is closest to everyday experience, and it is everyday experience, after all, that gives us reason (or not) to expend energy thinking about Christian teaching and Christian witness.[5] But if I am to communicate anything at all about the Christian life, I must speak of matters that will come up later in more detail. And later, when I address teaching and witness, I will develop ideas I have introduced in my remarks about the Christian life.

Each of the three main sections of the book, then, takes for granted what is said in the others. On every page, what I say harks back to a previous point or looks forward to a future one. I am always right in the middle of things. This is true even when I come to the end, because just there I need to go back to earlier chapters (or earlier writers!) to see what I can learn or what I need to revise. Except that I have to stop somewhere.

My point here is that neither I nor anyone else can ever say the *final* word. When Paul said, "We know only in part," he meant that human sight is always blurred. The God's-eye view is unattainable; we never get past the need to grow in understanding.[6] That's why I said this book is about *being and becoming* Adventist. We never arrive. At best, we only progress.

In February 1527, a group of Christian leaders who were determined to recover the spirit of the New Testament Christ gathered on a mountainside near Schleitheim, a town on the Swiss-German border. Medieval Christendom, with its alliance of prelates and princes, was tottering. Luther and Zwingli had ignited the Reformation, and those who met at Schleitheim were themselves children of that movement. But they wanted even deeper reform—less alignment with the political authorities, more alignment with Christ.

For having similar convictions, a friend of theirs, one Felix Manz, had already suffered execution by drowning. Their leader, Michael Sattler, had been banished from Zurich and Strasbourg. They were *Radical* Reformers. Less adventurous Christians, including those who exercised civil authority, looked at them askance.

The vision of these Radical Reformers was fragile and still in the making. They wanted to reach a clearer consensus about who they were and in that way to find new strength for Christian life and witness. Under Sattler's leadership, the participants settled on a method that one commentator called "the *dialogue of those concerned.*"[7] The point was to reach, through careful conversation, the kind of shared understanding that would build up the life of the church and enable its members to live out a deeper authenticity and faithfulness.

The conversation that took place at that gathering of Radical Reformers led to a statement of the group's shared belief. But no such statement can be final. What does withstand all criticism is the ideal of dialogue on the part of the concerned. Conversation is always crucial because growth is always necessary.

This book, a mere introduction, considers some Adventist basics and proposes a fresh perspective on those basics. My goal is simple: I wish to instigate further conversation. It's the ongoing conversation that, by God's grace, will open a window, or even a door, onto some deeper authenticity, some better way to live in the light of the Great Promise. You will have to see for yourself whether I succeed, whether anything here actually illuminates the experience of being and becoming Adventist.

What's certain is this: when you embrace the hope made known through Jesus, you set about looking for what God will next help you to become. Jesus' purpose, as He said in the Gospel of John, was that we should "have life, and have it abundantly"[8] And the full measure of that abundance lies always ahead of us on the journey of transformation that is God's call and God's gift to every human being.

---

1. From Jim Croce's "Bad, Bad Leroy Brown."

2. These classic Adventist words are from the concluding paragraph of Ellen White's *The Great Controversy* (Mountain View, Calif.: Pacific Press®, 1911), 678.

3. Karl Barth, *Church Dogmatics,* 2/1; trans. T. H. L. Parker, et al. (Edinburgh: T. & T. Clark, 1957), 250.

4. 1 Corinthians 4:7.

5. Here I have learned much from my late teacher James Wm. McClendon Jr. and from the outline of his three-volume *Systematic Theology,* published over the years 1986–2000 by Abingdon Press in Nashville.

6. The quoted phrase is from 1 Corinthians 13:9. The New Testament admonishes Christians to "grow in the grace and *knowledge* of our Lord and Savior Jesus Christ" (2 Peter 3:18; emphasis added).

7. My account of the Schleitheim meeting relies on the retelling in James Wm. McClendon Jr., *Systematic Theology,* vol. 1: *Ethics* (Nashville: Abingdon Press, 1986), 269–273. See page 270 for the quoted phrase.

8. John 10:10.

2

Reaching for Radical Hope

Serbs, Croats, and Muslims were in violent discord, and Bosnia was a rubble of broken hearts and dreams. Artillery and sniper fire, along with undependable roads and telephone lines, had isolated the three hundred thousand people in the Muslim-controlled section of Sarajevo, the capital.

It was 1992. That year the Adventist Development and Relief Agency, working with a tiny congregation, began hauling parcels of food into the most desperate section of the city. The food came mostly from refugee families trying to help their loved ones back home.

Word of the activity spread, and it wasn't long until Serb, Croat, and Muslim volunteers, hundreds of them, were using imported trucks to maintain an informal postal service between Sarajevo and safer cities elsewhere. Shipments came to a warehouse, where volunteers sorted it and posted address lists so recipients would know there were parcels for them. Other volunteers made deliveries to those too old or sick to leave their homes.

The trucks could pass through the Serb-controlled outskirts of Sarajevo only if the Serbs permitted it. The whole operation depended, in fact, on the cooperation and goodwill of the warring factions. A newspaper reporter found Milan Suslic, an Adventist pastor and relief agency director, and asked how members of the Sarajevo Adventist congregation were able to sustain the necessary cooperation and goodwill.

The pastor said they were "not part of any nationality or any side in the war"; they belonged "to the region, but not to the conflict." He said, too, that the makeshift postal service was fending off every hint of violence. "If somebody found even one bullet in a convoy," he explained, "our work would be ruined." And project leaders were putting constant effort into assuring the rival factions that the operation's aim was to help all groups in Sarajevo. In his most telling remark, Pastor Suslic declared, "We are nobody's and everybody's."

With these words, the pastor pictured a congregation that, in a world sundered by arrogance, would play no favorites and do no violence. For the purposes of their project, the congregation's members saw themselves as a people for all peoples, a source of blessing but not of discord. They simply wished the divine will done on earth as it is in heaven. They were few, but they would defy the stranglehold of violence. They would live out—today—the ideals that the Second Coming would establish forever.

By 1994, the informal postal service this congregation helped to lead had delivered some 500,000 letters and 350,000 packages.[1]

At the beginning of this church, near the midpoint of the nineteenth century, no Adventist could have imagined successors like those at Sarajevo. The first Adventists—the "pioneers"—were a tiny band, scattered here and there, without formal organization. Their world, in the northeast corner of the United States, was small; and their hope told them the end of time was so close that it made no sense to send missionaries overseas.

But if you look back from today to the story of the first Adventists, you see striking connections between them and the Sarajevo congregation. And these connections suggest that in the long conversation these pioneers began, Adventism has been reaching for a radical understanding of the Christian hope. It's a movement, in other words, that has been seeking the root, or original, meaning of a faith lived in the light of the Second Coming. The search matters because hope—out-of-the-ordinary hope—has been the church's identity from the start.

The story you will read here begins with a statement of simple loyalty to Christ, made when Adventists first began to link themselves together in a formal way. It traces the background of the statement and then developments from that point forward. You will see how, going forward and sometimes back, Adventists explored the true meaning of their loyalty to Christ. And you will see their hope beginning to fuse with the honoring of God's creation and concern for fullness of life on earth. More and more, it will become a summons to each of us to live our best and deepest dreams with confidence and courage.

The Beginning

Organized Adventism began in 1861, when a group of Seventh-day Adventist congregations in Michigan banded together as a legal association. The still-fledgling movement had been shaping its vision, its understanding of the Bible, for nearly twenty years. Delegates to this meeting had no interest, however, in a creedlike statement of belief. As James White said, a creed would block "new light" and stand in "direct opposition" to the "gifts" of the Holy Spirit. But the delegates did embrace a simple pledge: "We, the undersigned," they said, "hereby associate ourselves together as a church, taking the name, Seventh-day Adventists, covenanting together to keep the commandments of God and the faith of Jesus Christ."[2]

The pledge expressed the core convictions that united these early believers. Its key words brought to mind the parts of Scripture, such as Daniel and Revelation, in which vivid pictures and tumultuous drama highlight the urgency of faithfulness. And that urgency was in itself part of their story—a story that went back to the calculations of a man from upstate New York named William Miller.

Early in the nineteenth century, Miller devised an interpretation of predictions found in the book of Daniel and concluded that the second coming of Christ—God's final victory over evil—would occur in 1843 or 1844. Those who followed Miller finally settled on October 22 of the latter year. Although the Bible said no one would know the "day and hour"[3] of this event, the Millerites preached during a time when the then-dominant Protestant world was widely curious about signs of the

Second Coming. Their message was convincing enough to sweep throughout the northeastern United States.

On the predicted day, thousands stopped everything to look into the skies for Jesus' second coming. But they might as well have peered into the belly of the sea. The skies didn't light up, and the Advent failed to materialize. For those who had waited so eagerly, the effect was devastating. Their hopes "blasted," one man wrote, he and his friends "wept, and wept, till the day dawn."[4]

The Millerite interpretation had failed, and October 22, 1844, became the day of the Great Disappointment. Many lost faith, but the resilient held on, aching hearts and all, to the dream that Christ's appearing would happen soon. Among them were a few—Joseph Bates, James White, and Ellen Harmon the most influential—who began together a long journey of being and becoming Adventist. They kept their hope alive, and as understanding grew, began to revise it. Eventually, they began to focus on the practice of hope, the content of character, and the shape of daily life when you live by the light of the returning Christ.

Not that this could happen easily or quickly—not from the shadows of a broken dream. For a while, the resilient few continued to be so preoccupied with heaven that they showed little interest in earth or the quality of life on earth. James White and Ellen Harmon thought at first that it made no sense to marry; the world they knew would end too soon for that.

Even before the Great Disappointment, a few of those hoping for the Second Coming had considered and begun to keep the seventh-day Sabbath. But at a conference in upstate New York in early 1845, participants trying to make sense of their devastated hopes rebuffed this group and dismissed the Sabbath as being "Jewish." Joseph Bates, a retired sea captain, one-time prisoner of war, and committed antislavery activist, was not one to be cowed, however, by the prospect of controversy. The case for the Sabbath became compelling for him. He rushed to New Hampshire for an all-night study session with friends and emerged a Sabbath keeper.[5] Not long afterward, Ellen Harmon, by this time married to James, became convinced that Bates was right and gave her blessing to scriptural Sabbath keeping.

In the making now was a community that would embrace the hope of the Second Coming *while celebrating every week the goodness of creation, the value of human work, and the story of ancient Israel.* Adventists would begin to distance themselves from prejudice against the heritage of Judaism. And the Second Coming would find, through the Sabbath, a link to earthly yearnings and earthly possibilities.

By now these Adventists were already beginning to interpret their lives in terms of God's call for a "remnant"—a faithful minority, a courageous few—who would commit themselves to keeping the commandments of God and the faith of Jesus. The picture of the remnant was prominent in the Old Testament and enshrined anew in the visionary writings of John the revelator. Part of faithfulness, these pioneers came to believe, was honoring the Sabbath as God gave it. Part of it was allowing the whole life, teaching, and character of Christ to illuminate true faith.[6]

James and Ellen White established a magazine called *The Present Truth* in 1849, and still another, *The Advent Review,* in 1850. Now they were building their community. It was a community that could not be at one with a world unsympathetic to the teachings of Jesus. Some members, again with an ear to the book of Revelation, began expressing their disapproval of American slavery, even defying the 1850 Fugitive Slave Act by refusing to return runaway slaves and, in some cases, operating stations, or safe houses, on the Underground Railroad. At first, however, the only solution that they saw to the problem of slavery was the Second Coming. But one man, writing in the *Review,* objected that you should no more postpone a slave's freedom until the Second Coming than postpone your breakfast until then.[7] But more time would elapse before most Adventists would harness a sense of Christ's soon coming to a vision of human participation in the divine renewing of the world.

Still, Adventists were starting to see that hope must fit life on earth and a time that stretches out, and a consensus developed that congregations should organize as legal entities. So it was that in 1861, Michigan Adventists established a family, or "conference," of congregations, called themselves Seventh-day Adventists, and united under a covenant of faithfulness to the commandments of God and the faith of Jesus.

These pioneers shared a story of harrowing disappointment. Familiar, too, with the ordinary shocks that human flesh is heir to, they had still found in the story and joy of the gospel the strength to go on. Now, bearing witness to the triumph of hope over disappointment, their pledge was simple and direct: *they would honor God and follow Jesus in the company of others.* Under that pledge, solidarity with Christ was the key to the whole of life. You took the stories of God and Jesus to be one—loyalty to Jesus *was* loyalty to God—and you identified your whole being with that story. You made the risen and returning Christ your center, rule, and way; and you made His people your friends and fellowship.

Long before, Jesus Himself had hoped for the final victory of God. But the blessing of life on earth—life today—had been His passion, too. He had paid attention to the earth and had prayed that God's will be done here as in heaven. And if His was the root meaning of a faith lived in the light of hope, then radical hope *required* attention to the needs of today. With their covenant of faithfulness—that they would here and now follow Jesus as Lord—Adventists were finding their way to such a hope.

Aspiration and Adventure

In other states, congregations joined into conferences too. And in 1863, the entire family of Adventist churches organized under the name *General Conference of Seventh-day Adventists.* Although Adventists were putting down roots in a way the Millerites couldn't have imagined, the distance between their way of life and ordinary life remained. During the American Civil War, they were adamant in opposition to human slavery—it was a "sin of darkest dye," its perpetrators "dragon-hearted"—yet they held back from military service, putting the command of Jesus to love instead of kill the enemy above the pressure to do otherwise.[8]

After the war, Adventist life-enhancing institutions began to spring up. Years earlier, Joseph Bates had sworn off liquor and tobacco, and Ellen White, the visionary whose prophetic leadership would steer the church for decades, had addressed overindulgence and even the advantages of a vegetarian diet. In 1866, against that background, the first Adventist healthcare entity, the Western Health Reform Institute, began to operate in Battle Creek, Michigan. Eight years later, Adventist higher education began when Battle Creek College became a legal entity. Eight years after that, in 1882, a college opened in California, and a school that would become a college opened in Massachusetts.

Meanwhile, time on earth began to seem adequate for the opening of overseas missionary work, even though this had once seemed unnecessary. First, a former Polish priest, Michael Czechowski, made an unofficial journey to Europe. Then, in 1874, J. N. Andrews traveled there as the church's first official missionary. Within three decades, Adventists had taken their vision to every continent except Antarctica.

Back in America, a few women—with official licenses that challenged the convention of a masculine gospel ministry—joined the men who were trying, through evangelism, to widen the Adventist circle. In the 1880s, the circle grew more diverse when Edson White, the son of James and Ellen and a man courageous enough to face hostility and violence, went by river into the deep American South in order to evangelize former slaves and their sons and daughters.

Adventists were at the same time cooperating with people outside their circle in efforts of life-enhancing reform. Early in the nineteenth century, a culture of drinking—whiskey, rum, and hard cider were favorites—had taken an alarming toll on families, job performance, public safety, and even the integrity of politics. National worry had shaped itself into the temperance movement, and not long after Adventist conferences organized in the early 1860s, some members, including Ellen White, were encouraging one another to influence public policy through votes on the movement's behalf. When, in 1876, John Harvey Kellogg, the genius physician and inventor, took leadership of the institute that became better known as the Battle Creek Sanitarium, he championed Adventist involvement in the temperance movement. A few years later, Battle Creek elected an Adventist mayor who had campaigned on a temperance platform.

In the 1880s, Adventists fought hard to fend off Sunday laws that would have forced people throughout the country to stop work and close their businesses on Sunday. Besides hardship for anyone who dissented from the reigning Protestant orthodoxy, the laws would have undermined the separation of church and state that had long protected religious freedom in America. Early in the decade, Ellen White challenged students of Battle Creek College with the thought that they could "sit in deliberative and legislative councils," helping to enact the nation's laws.[9] In 1885, the General Conference president encouraged Arkansas Adventists who had been arrested for working on Sunday in their state to go to jail rather than pay their fines. In 1889, the church's National Religious Liberty Association declared that in resisting religious legislation, the church would come to the aid of "persecuted people of any race, color or creed."[10]

It was perhaps inevitable that Adventism's focus on the *practice* of hope would engender both anxiety and self-satisfaction. Existence formed by the vision of the returning Christ and the call to faithfulness in daily life could lapse easily into alarm about not being good enough for God. You could sense a need to be fully faithful, or even perfect, and then, falling short, feel anxious about measuring up to God's expectations. Or you could make Adventism's pledge of full loyalty to Christ a matter of conceit. You could succeed enough in your commitment to marvel at your strengths and overlook your weaknesses and begin to think of yourself as superior to others. One person, of course, could fall into both of these snares and have a weirdly conflicted inner life—a mishmash of self-loathing and self-adulation.

In 1888, at a meeting in Minneapolis, church leaders heard a contentious debate that grew out of these unhappy possibilities. In the end, the debate renewed their sense, on the one hand, of human inadequacy, and, on the other, of sheer gratitude for God's acceptance and good favor. The church was reminded that a person's "righteousness"—and as we might also say, a person's self-esteem—is by faith: we are forgiven and empowered by the grace of Christ. You don't earn God's approval, as religious "legalists" try to do. You simply benefit from God's grace—God's forgiveness and empowering presence. And at every step, you remain profoundly thankful for the ability this gives you to live your life with confidence.

That message of 1888, though sometimes resisted, would never lose its relevance. It was underscored a decade later when Ellen White, herself invigorated by the 1888 meeting, shared her own grace-centered experience in *The Desire of Ages,* a moving and widely circulated account of Jesus' life and ministry.

At the same time, Ellen White was continuing to refine her vision of cosmic struggle between good and evil, what she called the "great controversy" between Christ and Satan. The long arc of rebellion and renewal in God's universe brought to light three themes crucial for understanding the human story: the value of freedom, the importance of dissent, and the need for the Second Coming. Under its call to be the remnant—the dissenting faithful—the church was to confront evil through service and witness. It was to assist the poor and oppressed and to understand that "degradation" of a single individual means "loss" to everyone. Against abusive power and compromised religion, it was to declare a message of warning, correction, and hope.[11]

Ellen White died in 1915. A woman in a world dominated by men, she had been, by far, the most influential of the Adventist pioneers. Again and again she had authorized innovation; again and again she had endorsed the founding of colleges and other institutions. Her witness, built on a hope framed by the festival of Sabbath, had galvanized a whole community to aspiration and adventure.

Caution, Then New Adventure

With the voice of Ellen White silent and the wider Christian community skittish from evolution and other cultural developments, Adventism became, in certain respects, less daring. Fortunately, evangelism flourished, spurred on by the three angels' messages of Revelation 14 and the call to saintly "endurance" in a time of pervasive homage to evil power. Moreover, the church did keep some distance from nationalism and did continue to uphold religious liberty. In 1921, the Autumn Council of church leaders even issued a statement expressing loyalty to "the Prince of Peace." In this statement, they spoke out against the federal government's spending of "vast sums for armaments of war" when the money could be "devoted to the amelioration of human woe and the advancement of peaceful pursuits."[12]

But over the several decades leading up to the 1960s, the journey of becoming Adventist—of searching always for new vision and deeper authenticity—gave way to preoccupation with what had been achieved so far. Most of the church's energy went into shoring up institutional strength and beliefs and into securing wider acceptance. During the Nazi period, a courageous Adventist named John Weidner—now listed in a place of honor at the Holocaust Museum in Washington, D.C.—helped numerous Jews escape Adolf Hitler's web of hate. But what he did was exceptional, and the prevailing tendency—inward focus, misgivings about risk, desire for acceptance—carried a price: Adventist leaders in Germany itself, with no reproof from elsewhere in the church to disturb them, repeatedly expressed their support for Hitler.[13]

In the 1950s, Adventist leaders hoping for affirmation entered into an exchange with two prominent evangelical writers. The exchange was controversial and kicked off new discussion on the themes of human inadequacy and divine grace that had come up in 1888. Soon afterward, the civil rights movement, with its cry for racial justice, brought America's injustice—and pent-up anger—to the foreground. In 1965, in the midst of the controversy, the *Review and Herald* said Adventist efforts to influence public policy concerning race were "strictly out of bounds" and would waste the church's moral authority on matters irrelevant to "the gospel commission." But the diversity that had come into the church with the mission to Black America in the 1880s now paid dividends. The church's magazine for Black evangelism gave careful support to cooperative Christian action on the matter of race relations, and in 1969, the influential African American evangelist E. E. Cleveland declared that "passivism" regarding sociopolitical problems is an evil. Those, he said, who call for disengagement from social concerns are "purveyors of misery" and "are not the servants of God."[14]

Now the journey of becoming—the *adventure* of truth—came into prominence again. Those uncomfortable with the journey would repeatedly contest it, but it never rolled to a halt. Through the rest of the twentieth century, Adventists searching for deeper authenticity engaged one another on numerous issues, including once again the question of "righteousness by faith" that had led to the 1888 discussion in Minneapolis. Discussion ranged now over a wide array of subjects, and often from perspectives at once fresh and, for many, disconcerting. Church members began looking, for example, at the interpretation of the Bible, the shape of the Adventist lifestyle, the nature of Ellen White's prophetic leadership, the meaning of the Sabbath and Second Coming, the significance of Daniel and Revelation, the question of God and human freedom, the place of women in a truly biblical community, the conduct of mission, the responsibility of the church for society, and the relevance of peacemaking in Adventist witness. The conversations were lively and sometimes contentious, and shortfalls of truthfulness and imagination loomed as large as the breakthroughs. Still, the conversations were often energizing.

Seventh-day Adventists in the 1960s and thereafter were aware of imperfection and restless for growth, as thriving communities must be. With many of them alive in thought and hope alike, their practice of the Christian life was undergoing transformation too. A student missionary program was invented. Healthcare institutions grew in number and in influence. The Adventist Development and Relief Agency took innovative and well-funded compassion to sites around the world. The Center for Law and Public Policy, near Washington, D.C., galvanized the wider religious community for struggle against the murderous tobacco industry. All the while, but especially as the twentieth century gave way to the twenty-first, the church was exploding with new converts overseas and contending for new strength in the older, wealthier—and now too-often-stagnant—strongholds of America, Western Europe, and Australia.

All this was faith's struggle, inside of Adventism, to address the yearnings of the human heart. It was adventurous. It was out of the ordinary. It was a people's often brash, sometimes halting, effort to flourish—to be fully alive—in God's world.

In 1980, in the midst of all this, church leaders, skittish about turmoil, voted a lengthy statement of official Adventist belief. The statement harked back, in some ways, to the period after Ellen White, when the church's energy went into shoring up what had been achieved in the past. Still, the "preamble" said that under the guidance of the Holy Spirit, new understanding could be "expected."[15] The 1980 document was not the final word. The journey of *becoming*—of searching always for new vision and deeper authenticity—would go on.

As the twentieth century was careening to its end, the Adventist community in South Africa was fragile from the years of pain and distrust associated with apartheid, or government-enforced racial separation. But South African apartheid crumbled, and the nation's new leaders set up a Truth and Reconciliation Commission so that citizens could confess responsibility and remorse for what they had contributed to a long nightmare of violence and injustice. Adventists wondered what to do.

In 1998, after protracted and difficult conversation, they responded with an official statement of confession. The confession began with words from Revelation about the fully faithful, those who at all times and under any hardship "keep the commandments of God and hold fast to the faith of Jesus." This fragment of Scripture is the same that had in 1861 bound Michigan's pioneering Adventists together in a pledge to honor God and follow Jesus in the company of others.

Now these words—these signature words for the community of hope that is Seventh-day Adventism—gave voice to collective sorrow and gave direction for a new commitment. In a place raw with hurt and desperate for renewal, Adventists declared their allegiance to nothing less than "reformation, justice and reconciliation" in South Africa. It was a human declaration, no doubt imperfect in both its expression and its sincerity. But in reach and aspiration, it was breathtaking.[16]

The Millerites—and Seventh-day Adventists at the very start—could not have envisioned such a thing, any more than they could have envisioned the postal service in ravaged Sarajevo. But along with their hope, Adventists had embraced the call to keep the commandments of God and the faith of Jesus. And if at first their eyes couldn't see the fusing of hope with concern for fullness of life, our eyes *can.* Ours can see that for the blessing of the earth and of the here-and-now that God has made, hope and covenant faithfulness—a striving after Jesus' goals by the faith that He lived out—go together.

This is so because in both being *and* becoming Adventist, the pioneers not only held on to their faith, but they enhanced it—enhanced understanding and practice alike. And for all the differences between now and then, the connections remain, plain as the shining sun.

Today, the vision of the Adventist pioneers—and their urgency in the face of Christ's return—brings comfort to human hearts, as it always has. What is more, it shapes both the will and the imagination for tasks that lie at hand. It builds lives on earth. It renews the world. It has begun to be—now and then and here and there—not mere hope but *radical* hope, the hope that came to be through Jesus, a hope lived out against convention, a hope lived out on earth.

But behind the Adventist story is a master story that is the compass and inspiration for every Christian and every Christian people. That is what we turn to now.

---

1. James Rupert, "Neither Shells nor Gloom of War Stays Group From Aiding Sarajevo," *The Washington Post,* June 24, 1993, A29, 30. Ralph Watts, then ADRA president, shared these statistics in personal conversation on April 9, 1994. Charles Sandefur, the current president, told me in 2004 that this account continues to appear to be well-founded.

2. The pledge is cited in *Seventh-day Adventist Encyclopedia* (Washington, D.C.: Review and Herald®, 1966), 310. One account of the meeting, including the discussion of creeds that preceded embrace of the pledge, is in Arthur L. White, *Ellen G. White: The Early Years, 1827–1862* (Washington, D.C.: Review and Herald®, 1985), 453, 454.

3. Matthew 24:36.

4. Quoted in Douglas Morgan, *Adventism and the American Republic* (Knoxville, Tenn.: University of Tennessee Press, 2001), 3.

5. See R. W. Schwarz, *Light Bearers to the Remnant* (Mountain View, Calif.: Pacific Press®, 1979), 54, 59, 60.

6. For this latter, see P. Gerard Damsteegt, *Foundations of the Seventh-day Adventist Message and Mission* (Grand Rapids, Mich.: Eerdmans, 1977), 192–194. Here the author quotes both James and Ellen White.

7. Anson Byington; his exact words are quoted in Morgan, 28.

8. Comments of Ellen White and Uriah Smith, cited in Morgan, 28, 29.

9. From White's *Fundamentals of Christian Education,* 82, this remark is quoted in Jonathan M. Butler, "Adventism and the American Experience," in Edwin S. Gaustad, ed., *The Rise of Adventism* (New York: Harper & Row, 1974), 195.

10. Quoted in Morgan, 47.

11. See Morgan, 56.

12. Quoted in Morgan, 105.

13. For an account of Weidner, see, e.g., Gay Block and Malka Drucker, *Rescuers: Portraits of Moral Courage in the Holocaust* (New York: TV Books, 1998), 80–85. For Adventist failure during the Nazi period, see, e.g., Erwin Sicher, "Seventh-day Adventist Publications and the Nazi Temptation," *Spectrum* 8 (1977): 11–24.

14. A long quote from the *Review* editorial may be found in Charles W. Teel Jr., ed., *Remnant & Republic: Adventist Themes for Personal and Social Ethics* (Loma Linda, Calif.: Loma Linda University Center for Christian Bioethics, 1995), 21; for the Black Adventist perspective, see Morgan, 160–162.

15. Malcolm Bull and Keith Lockhart, in the second edition of their *Seeking a Sanctuary: Seventh-day Adventism and the American Dream* (Bloomington, Ind.: Indiana University Press, 2006), 105–108, argue that a second fundamentalism (following the first that, in their account, emerged after the death of Ellen White) took root in 1980s and 1990s Adventism. The preamble to the 1980 Statement of Fundamental Beliefs remains a bulwark against sheer fundamentalism.

16. I have relied on John Webster, of La Sierra University, for the telling of this story.

3

The Story Behind the Story

In work and play and daydreams, thoughts come to us in the form of stories. As a child, you play house, imagine bloody conflicts, dream of batting in the winning run. If you become an entrepreneur, you plot scenarios for business success. When you are a grandmother, you remember birthday parties and make plans for the beginning, middle, and ending of Christmas dinner.

The self you share with friends and loved ones or mull over when you tote up your failures and accomplishments is constructed out of the stories you live and live by. You are a comedy and a drama all in one: here a pratfall, there a moment of glory; here a rejection, there a romance; here bewilderment, there a life mission. And as your life unfolds, the stories you dwell on—your own, your family's, what you pick up from news, fairy tales, or video games—govern your dreams and daily life. The characters you identify with—most admire, most want to imitate—shape you into the kind of person you are turning out to be.

When you live as a Christian and undertake the journey of transformation that is Adventism, you make one story the master story of your life. It matters more to you than any episode in sports or business; any hero, celebrity, or character of literature; any workplace; any political or religious institution. The center of that master story—the grand ideal it

34

all leads up to—is Jesus of Nazareth. Its beginning is Abraham, the father of the movement Jesus loved and wanted to advance.

The first great champions of the Good News about the risen Jesus were Peter and Stephen. According to the New Testament, the early Christian believers gathered around their testimony and marveled at their courage and persuasive power. Both of them, it turns out, explained their commitment to Jesus with reference to the story of the Jews and the call of Abraham. God had told Abraham to leave home for a new land and had promised that his descendants would be a blessing to people everywhere.[1] Jesus was the key, they believed, to the fulfillment of that promise.

The Family History

It's amazing that Abraham, the father of the Hebrew people, actually went.[2] Before he began to trust God and set out on his journey, human beings thought nothing new—nothing really new—could ever happen. The stories people told in his day were long complaints about a fate that was written in the stars and couldn't be changed. Abraham came after the Sumerians, a cultured and inventive people, the makers of early civilization. But the Sumerians didn't think they could make a truly important difference. When Gilgamesh, their legendary hero, was nearing the end of his life, he doubted that there was any point to exerting oneself. "You only fill your flesh with grief," he said.[3]

Abraham thought you *could* make a difference. You weren't trapped by the whims of coldhearted deities but belonged to a God who took an interest in you and who was able, at every turn, to transform human possibilities. The God who addressed Abraham would make of his seed a " 'great nation,' " and would not only bless that nation but would also make it a blessing for others. In and through Abraham, God had said, " 'all the families of the earth shall be blessed.' "[4]

This was the Great Promise: the assurance of universal blessing, of a day when everyone will flourish and everyone be fully alive. But it was impossible—or must have seemed so. Still, from then to now, Abraham's children, or the best of them, have said Yes to impossible dreams. In the culture of Jewish faith, you live that way: you pursue goals that seem impossibly far in front of you. Sure, you do acknowledge setbacks; you face reality, and you don't lose yourself in some Pollyanna fantasy. But you never give up. Again and again, you say Yes. The promise behind all this was unearned, an expression of God's sheer generosity.

Later, after many family wanderings and an unexpected descent into Egyptian slavery, Abraham's children again felt the imprint of divine generosity. Now called Israelites, they were aliens in Egypt, wretched and bent under the forced labor and ceaseless fear that came from the hand of Pharaoh. Hearing their cry, God came to Moses and announced a divine deliverance: God would send Moses to Egypt, and he would be the people's liberator.

So, was it God or Moses who would provide deliverance? It's best, perhaps, to say that it would take place because God was working in partnership with Moses, and Moses in partnership with God. In any case, the Hebrew Bible recounts a remarkable escape from Egypt, and it wasn't long until the Israelites were encamped on the far side of the Red Sea, near Mount Sinai.

Here God renewed the pledge, or "covenant," made with Israel's father, Abraham. With Moses as spokesperson, God reminded the people of how " 'I bore you on eagles' wings' " out of Egyptian slavery. Now, by taking the road God would lead them on, they could be, together, their Maker's representative on earth, and could both experience and share the blessings of intimacy with God. In other words, they could be a "priestly kingdom and a holy nation"—they could bring God to others by being faithful.[5]

This was a reaffirmation of the adventure Abraham was offered. Hearing it, the people were now ready to receive from God the Ten Commandments. In these commandments, they saw again how God had liberated them from slavery, and before that had made the heavens and the earth for everyone to share. In expressing how they could live responsibly, the commandments recalled the Sabbath, affirming the sacred celebration that would always signal both the closeness and the partnership

God and humanity were meant to enjoy.

At Mount Sinai, the call to be a blessing was seen in light of God's own initiative for suffering Israel.[6] As God came to Israel's aid, so, henceforth, would Israel come to the aid of others. Sabbath celebration would be for everyone, aliens included; oppression would be forbidden; widows and orphans would be cared for. In its details, the Sinai moral code would later need amendment, most famously by Jesus Himself; but the basic vision of fair play and special regard for the poor came clearly into view.

According to the Bible, Israel vowed to live as God was asking them to live—vowed to *be* God's human partner. And after long years in the wilderness, Abraham's children finally did cross the river Jordan into Canaan. Here, in the Promised Land they'd set their hopes on, life was better. Yet all too often it was still tumultuous and violent.

Again and again the people veered off the road God wanted them to walk. In due course, they came under the rulership of kings. One of these kings, David, would become a lasting symbol of the just and peaceful governance that would bring to grand fulfillment the pledge God gave Abraham. Still, most of Israel's kings tilted into arrogance and made the poor and sorrowing feel worse than before. Eventually, the people, aggrieved, impatient, and forgetful of their shared story, split in two and began to live under the skittish oversight of competing kings. In the end, they fell victim to foreign powers, and some made forced marches into servitude and exile.

Amid chaos and wrenching loss, prophets arose, thundering words of rebuke, moral vision, and great hope. These prophets—Amos, Isaiah, Zechariah, and the like—expanded on the dream that Abraham had lived by. They said action for others, not words and rituals, mattered most to God. They upheld compassion, spoke for victims, and said the workers and the poor deserved just treatment. They declared that no setback could defeat God's promise.

One of the greatest of the prophets, Jeremiah, became, as one historian remarked, the "first Jew"—*Jew*, that is, in the sense we are familiar with today. Jeremiah died in Egypt, uprooted from home as a result of a Babylonian invasion. He not only spent some of his life outside the

Promised Land but also reflected on how to be faithful when you do. He told those of his people who ended up in Babylon to build houses, bear children, and "seek the welfare of the city" you reside in. This last was especially generous and set a standard for how to be Jewish away from home. But Jeremiah's generosity was not blind: do not, he said, embrace Babylonian dreams instead of God's.

Since Jeremiah's day, being a descendant of Abraham yet living outside the Promised Land has become so commonplace that now it is what the term *Jew* usually suggests. Jeremiah argued that when you are faithful in this condition, you are *in* but not wholly *of* the culture where you find yourself. You belong to a separate people, yet you seek the betterment of the whole community.[7]

The songwriter John Lennon asked everyone to "imagine all the people / Living life in peace." Long centuries before, so did Ezekiel, another of the great prophets. Ezekiel was familiar with humiliation. He himself saw Babylonian invaders destroy Jerusalem; he himself served his displaced people in a foreign land. Yet he was confident enough to hold on to the promise God had given Abraham and to describe it, unforgettably, as a "covenant of peace." The phrase was as winsome as August rain, and the theme of peace would later epitomize the gospel vision. God's blessing would take the shape of peace, or, in Hebrew, *shalom*. In other words, it would bring food, freedom, and safety—prosperity and well-being; the conditions for human flourishing—to everyone.[8]

The prophets knew well that God's people bore hardship and pain, often undeserved. But they continued, the best of them, to believe that blessing for everyone really meant *everyone*. In Jerusalem, Isaiah had imagined a day when Egypt, Assyria, and Israel, though enemies prone to hatred and horrific bloodshed, would one day worship together, a community of nations equally blessed and fully reconciled.[9]

Later, in the Servant Songs, the prophet saw a world united against Israel, and Israel refusing to retaliate. But with startling generosity and hope, he declared that Israel's wounds would somehow have healing effect, somehow bring about peace and well-being in the world. It was a vision that anticipated the Jesus story: nonviolence and suffering could be redemptive and clear the way to something better. The covenant of peace would hold through all the ups and downs, and God's people would help bring ruin to repair.[10]

The Jesus Story

According to the Bible, Israel did survive, sometimes flourishing and sometimes not; sometimes rebuilding cities, sometimes facing new catastrophe. Jesus, who would become the focus of Christian faith, was born at a point of the nation's deep humiliation. The Roman Empire held sway in the land. The streets were bristling with foreign soldiers. The Roman authorities were coldhearted, often ferocious. The Jews themselves, understandably, were on edge, some cooperating with the enemy, some resisting, some just trying to make do. As may happen in any tradition, religious leaders all too often busied themselves with mere piety and focused more on themselves than on the poor and the sorrowing.

Ordinary folk—especially the neediest—were desperate for change.

In childhood, Jesus learned and loved the Jewish heritage. At about the age of thirty, He came under the influence of John the Baptist, a desert preacher, and soon afterward embarked on a public mission that would endear Him to the vulnerable and leave the authorities, Roman and Jewish alike, indignant and revengeful. It wasn't long until He was arrested and killed. The story could have ended there, but, in fact, it was just beginning.

Like Abraham, Jesus, when His mission began, had left His hometown and took to the road. With a growing band of followers, He visited villages around the Sea of Galilee and then regions to the northwest and southeast of the sea. In time, He and His followers turned their faces farther south, to Jerusalem, their culture's capital.

All along Jesus lived as a Jew, loving the heritage that made Him who He was. But He was a radical Jew. He said a new day was dawning and asked people to open their hearts and change their minds. He shared maxims and stories you could never forget. He healed sick people and forgave the guilty. Like the prophets before Him, He made outsiders into insiders, argued with the high and mighty, and set forth a vision of prosperity and well-being for all. When He spelled out His take on the future, His predictions were unsettling yet profoundly hopeful.

In Jesus' first sermon, given on a Sabbath and recorded in the Gospel of Luke, He rolled out His mission with words from Isaiah. God has sent me, He said, "to bring good news to the poor." My work is "to proclaim release to the captives and recovery of sight to the blind" and "to let the oppressed go free."[11]

As for those who would follow Him, Jesus described their life and mission in the longest of His recorded sermons. Found in Matthew 5 through 7, it is a fresh interpretation of the vision caught by Abraham and of the road laid down at Sinai.

"Blessed" are you disciples, Jesus said from the mountain where He had sat down with them. When you know your need, show compassion to others, become peacemakers, suffer persecution for doing what is right, you will receive gifts that are fitting for you. You can rejoice, therefore, and be glad. And in the blessedness you enjoy, you can be a blessing too. "You are the salt of the earth," enhancing human life. "You are the light of the world," showing the way to God.

When you truly follow Me, Jesus continued, you are generous in heart—always. Even when enemies mistreat you, you do no violence against them but hold your ground with creative love. Like the God whose sun and rain nourish both the "evil" and the "good," you show unfailing concern for others, pray even for your persecutors. All the while, you make no vain show of piety or goodness. Your only passion is the divine will, done "on earth as it is in heaven." Your only security is the God who "gives good things" to those who ask.

What falls short of all this, Jesus said to conclude, is false and leads to ruin. But when you live in accordance with it, you are like a wise man who builds his house on a rock: in wind and flood alike, you are unassailable.

It was a radical vision based on a radical hope. Both human hearts and human institutions would be transformed. By means of compassion as ecumenical as dawn—reaching out to friend and foe alike—God's joyous few would break the stranglehold of violence and turn the world toward peace. This would be difficult, of course, and in Luke's account of Jesus, Christian life is a matter of prayer and compassion combined. Meeting human need sends you to your knees; prayer gives you strength to renew the effort.[12]

From the start, Jesus Himself encountered difficulty. The goal of peace on earth—blessing that reaches out to everyone—is disturbing to those who, by luck, labor, or both, and often by violence, acquire flagrant wealth and power. Even at His first sermon, so Luke tells us, some of the townspeople seized Jesus and tried to throw Him off a cliff. But ordinary folk warmed to His mission, finding in His words and manner solace for raw sorrows and passion for new dreams. When their fervor intensified and their number grew, the authorities took fretful notice. Finally, in Jerusalem, they came after Jesus, brought Him to trial, and had Him executed in the Roman fashion: He was crucified—nailed to a wooden post and crossbar and left to weaken and finally to suffocate.

Except for a few women and a thief who had asked for His blessing, Jesus at His darkest moment had no human companionship. Still, in the spirit of His own teaching, He looked at His executioners and at the scoffers standing by and prayed, " 'Father, forgive them; for they do not know what they are doing.' "[13]

Shortly afterward, He was dead.

The Witnesses

In a matter of days, however, Peter, a disciple who during Jesus' trial had deserted Him, was standing before a large Jerusalem crowd and announcing his conviction that Jesus was, in fact, alive. With a nod to believing friends who were with him, he declared, " 'This Jesus God raised up, and of that all of us are witnesses.' " So everyone, he continued, should " 'know with certainty that God has made him both Lord and Messiah, this Jesus whom you crucified.' "[14]

As Jesus had done, Peter and his co-believers invited all who would listen to open their hearts. The risen Jesus, they said, was Messiah, or

Christ—the Cornerstone of a movement that would be, for all time, the key to human flourishing, the means to peace on earth.[15] They urged every listener to acknowledge Him and to join the movement they were starting.

Like Jesus, the first witnesses to the resurrection embraced their Jewish heritage. But like Jesus, they also met with antagonism as well as approval. Some were arrested. Stephen was the first to die a martyr. But as he was being stoned to death, he displayed the solidarity with Christ that would become the hallmark of the true disciple: instead of spewing hate, he echoed the prayer the dying Jesus had offered for His enemies. " 'Lord,' " he said, " 'do not hold this sin against them.' "[16]

Saul, who would one day become the apostle Paul, stood at the site, approving Stephen's execution. Then, driven by religious fervor, he resumed his own campaign of intimidation, breaking into Christian houses and breathing "threats and murder against the disciples of the Lord."[17] He continued to think his violence was the will of God until one day, on the road to Damascus, he himself faced the risen Jesus as Peter and his friends had done. Taken aback, he began a turnaround, spending time with those he formerly had hated and reassessing everything. No Christian took revenge against him, and in a few years, his energy rechanneled, he became the first missionary, crossing land and sea to share the good news of Jesus' resurrection.

Paul, as he was now called, spent the rest of his life in a succession of great cities, starting conversations in the synagogues and marketplaces, organizing churches, and writing letters to keep those churches faithful and full of confidence. To him, the resurrection meant that Christ is God's human face, the medium of grace and peace. It meant that everyone is equal. It meant that nothing matters more than love, and nothing can defeat love.

Others joined the chorus of affirmation, some leading churches, some writing Gospels and letters and the dark poetry of hope you find in such a book as Revelation. Many became ordinary members of Christian congregations, taking new ideals into daily life and struggling to uphold them. All knew the single conviction that gave them common ground:

God had shone through human lives before, but Jesus alone bore the "exact imprint" of the Divine.[18]

By the year 100, some seventy-five hundred people were Christians. Most lived in cities, and many were well educated. Compared to the average of the day, their generosity was startling, and through person-to-person influence over decade after decade, their number grew, by the fourth century, to half the population of the Roman Empire.[19]

The church's expansion was swift. As for authenticity, however, there were both gains and losses. Martyrs and other saints gave Christians exemplary lives to whet imagination and inspire faithfulness. Translators brought the Bible to new peoples and weakened the dominion of Roman culture. But at the same time, the church drifted from its Jewish roots and began a long slide toward accommodation with the imperial power. In the early fourth century, Constantine, the Roman emperor, declared himself a Christian. He gave imperial endorsement to Sunday, a Sabbath different from that of the Jews. With further, and still more stunning, disregard for the Jesus story, he made the cross a battlefield banner. Christians by now were largely recanting their refusal of violence; now, when it appeared "just" to do so, ordinary members (though not the clergy) could strap on the weapons of war.

Over the ensuing centuries, the church continued to grow. But members paid less attention now to the gospel story proper and more attention to ideas and arguments you could grasp whether you knew the story or not. At the same time, they became less interested in how people lived together and more focused on the inner life: on right belief, on purity of conscience, on facing shortcomings and dealing with guilt.

By the time of Martin Luther, the sixteenth-century Reformer, obsession with inner life and especially inner failure was at fever pitch. Luther embodied that obsession, and he responded to it. His great gift to the church, formed in large part by new attention to Bible study, was a liberating awareness of God's forgiving generosity, or grace.

With some Christians in Luther's wake, notably the Anabaptists of Switzerland, Germany, and Holland, this sense of grace, combined with the recovery of Bible study, made for new awareness of the gospel story.

And with that came not just a road to inner serenity but also the rediscovery of discipleship and of Christlike peacemaking as a gospel ideal.

These Christians, known today as Radical Reformers, took Luther's sense of divine forgiveness and made it, as in the church's beginning, the benchmark for right relationships with people. The blessing God promised at the start was not just "peace of mind" but the sweeping wholeness of life that the prophets spoke about and Jesus died defending. Divine forgiveness—not just received but also embodied in the Christian community—would provide the foothold for finding the way to such wholeness of life.

These same Radical Reformers objected to "Christendom"—the long habit, stretching back to Constantine, of seeing the church and the state as one and the same. You were not a Christian, they said, just because you were born into a "Christian" state or a "Christian" civilization. With this in mind, they brought back the practice of adult baptism. The sprinkling of infants was misguided, a symbol of how true discipleship could be lost in a Constantinian fog. You were Christian, they believed, because you had made a thoughtful, voluntary commitment to follow Jesus in the company of others. You were Christian because you made your loyalty to Jesus higher than any other—higher even than your loyalty to your tribe or nation.

Today the struggle for Christian authenticity goes on. The dominant culture's suspicion of traditional authority and glorification of self-interest make the struggle difficult. What is more, the world, for all its beauty and bounty, is still dangerous, still fractured by the very greed it lionizes, still resistant to human goodness. Self-indulgence is one thing; when joined to the loss of hope that persistent pain may generate, it heightens even more the temptation to give up on the Great Promise, and to give in to another ethos, one that denies the possibility of peace through generosity.

The struggle for authenticity requires, then, ever more diligent attention to the story—the *master* story—of the Christian life. That master story is what underlies the story of Adventism, and what provides the true compass and inspiration for each new turn in its development.

If by God's grace you can see yourself as a character in that story and can identify with Abraham and others in the story, and especially with

Jesus, who alone is the "exact imprint" of the Divine, you are ready to live as a Christian and to undertake the journey that is Adventism. You are ready to look again, every day, at who you are, and ready, every day, to make adjustments for the better.

You are ready, in short, not only to receive, but also to *be,* a blessing.

---

1. For Peter's remark, see Acts 3:13–15; for Stephen's, see Acts 7:2, 3. Both preachers refer to a story in Genesis 12:1–4.

2. Genesis 12:4. At this point in Genesis, of course, Abraham is still called Abram.

3. Thomas Cahill recounts and interprets the *Epic of Gilgamesh* in his *The Gifts of the Jews* (New York: Doubleday, 1998), 20–39. The quote is from page 36.

4. Genesis 12:2, 3.

5. Exodus 19:4, 6.

6. The so-called book of the covenant is chapters 19–24 of Exodus.

7. See Jeremiah 29:1–9. For this interpretation of Jeremiah and of Diaspora Judaism, I rely on James Wm. McClendon Jr., *Doctrines: Systematic Theology*, vol. 2 (Nashville: Abingdon, 2002), 355, 356. McClendon cites historian Paul Johnson's description of Jeremiah as the "first Jew."

8. This view of the promise—this vision of peace—is in Ezekiel 34:25–31.

9. Isaiah 19:23–25.

10. From the Servant Songs; see Isaiah 42:3; 50:5, 6; and all of chapter 53, especially verse 12. *See also* Isaiah 54:10—"my covenant of peace shall not be removed, says the LORD"—and Isaiah 61:4.

11. Luke 4:18, 19, alluding to words in Isaiah 61:1, 2, and 58:6.

12. I paraphrase Thomas Cahill, *Desire of the Everlasting Hills* (New York: Nan A. Talese/Anchor Books, 1999), 190.

13. Luke 23:34.

14. Acts 2:32, 36.

15. Luke, who wrote Acts, the history of the first believers, puts the theme of peace "on earth" (Luke 2:14) into the mouth of the angels who sang for the shepherds at Jesus' birth. In Acts 10:36, he has Peter saying that God's message is "peace by Jesus Christ."

16. Acts 7:60.

17. Acts 8; 9 tell the story of Paul's conversion.

18. Hebrews 1:3.

19. Here I rely on sociologist Rodney Stark in *The Rise of Christianity* (Princeton, N.J.: Princeton University Press, 1996), chapters 1 and 2.

4

The Adventist Way

After the long night of apartheid in South Africa, you could finally see the colors of dawn. It was 1993, Nelson Mandela was out of jail, and the first free and fair elections were just around the corner.

That was when Ginn Fourie's life took an agonizing turn. A Seventh-day Adventist mother, she found out one heart-stopping night that Lyndi, her only daughter, was dead, killed in a massacre. Lyndi had been a student at the University of Capetown. Along with three other students, she'd been shot by gunmen from the Pan Africanist Congress. All the victims were unknown to the assailants.

Almost immediately, Ginn Fourie determined that she would absorb this evil without passing it on. At the funeral, she read a prayer she'd written and stunned everyone by quoting a prayer Jesus prayed while He was on the cross: " 'Father forgive them for they do not know what they do.' " Later, she met her daughter's killers both at their trial and at hearings conducted by the Truth and Reconciliation Commission of South Africa, and she expressed her forgiveness to them directly. Later still, she met with them in prison, urging them to take responsibility for what they had done and expressing once again her forgiveness.

Ginn Fourie had drawn her circle large enough to include people who didn't deserve to be there. Now she made forgiveness her mission. She accepted numerous invitations to tell her story. She befriended the mastermind who ordered the massacre, and, according to his testimony, helped him change his mind about meeting violence with violence. Along with him, she set up a foundation whose purpose is to advance reconciliation in South Africa.

The prayer at her daughter's funeral had ended on a note of hope. "I trust You with my precious Lyndi," Ginn Fourie had told God. Then, noting that this "planet is a dangerous place to live," she had expressed her confidence that Jesus would return. She understood that the Cross is not the end of the story Christians tell, and she understood that the returning Jesus is the very One who prayed for the well-being of His executioners. This Jesus was the content of her hope, and it was a hope she was going to put into practice that day and every day thereafter.[1]

Sabbath and the Practice of Hope

The Adventist way is the practice of hope. It came into being, as it turns out, with the discovery of the Sabbath.

Finding a path for living—and living well—is everyone's obsession. Dreaming about where life will take you can be as exhilarating as a breeze across a bay. But disappointments happen, and you become acquainted with the anxieties and raw sorrows that afflict the human heart. Then you wonder how to mend a broken life, and how to live when brokenness never completely goes away.

When you are caught between your dreams and disappointments, how in the world can you flourish? The Adventist way speaks to this yearning. It is a journey of hope, defined in large part by thoughts of new life and by attitudes and actions that match those thoughts. Still, the Adventist way arose out of the Great Disappointment, and from the beginning, those who embraced it were familiar with shadow as well as sunshine. So when you are Adventist, you know peril and heartbreak just like everyone else. But even when you face the silence of God and weep until dawn, you smile through the tears. When you are Adventist, you keep faith in human possibility, celebrate the wonder and goodness of creation, and work for what you hope for. All that is what the *practice of*

47

hope is about. For the first Adventists, it was the Sabbath that made it come to life.

The Sabbath swept into early Adventist experience following the anguish of 1844, and, like a rainbow, it brought sheer rejuvenation. The first Adventists were wounded, and they had imperfect—even fearful—understandings of the human relationship with God. Still, the Sabbath they welcomed was the very festival of gladness God gave in the beginning. And with its signal of divine presence—divine-human *friendship*—it told Adventists what it had told the faithful in Jesus' day and before: You are precious in God's sight. You have God's creation to savor and appreciate. You have a mission that matters. You have friends to keep you company.

Both the hope of final victory for the risen Christ and the weekly celebration of the Sabbath remain to this day the insignia of Adventism, its keys for human flourishing. When by God's grace you embrace such a hope and participate in such renewing celebrations, you end up with a strong, true purpose and a heart both generous and glad.

Of course, the part about the Sabbath was more a recognition than a discovery. In the Bible, the Sabbath is as familiar as breath. According to Genesis, it was the capstone of Creation—the seventh day that gave meaning and direction to the other six, the promise that life wouldn't be frittered away by distraction or routine, the gift of rest and companionship and sheer enjoyment of creation. The Sabbath would keep you from sleepwalking through life: you would think about and enjoy the days and years God gave you. It would be time off from the commerce and clatter of the weekdays—a day "made," so Jesus declared, "for humankind." And the keeping of it, as the prophet said, would be a "delight."[2]

Knowing that work without rest is at once exhausting and dispiriting, God not only offered the gift of the Sabbath but also asked us to take advantage of it. The Sabbath was at once both an opportunity and a discipline. In keeping it, the goodness of creation would come through, and also the possibility of new life—both as plain as the shining sun. Remember the Sabbath, God said, because I made "heaven and earth, the sea, and all that is in them." Observe it because I gave you a new start—

"brought you out" of Egyptian slavery "with a mighty hand and an out-stretched arm."[3]

No hostile or indifferent power made the world, and no hostile or indifferent power could keep humanity forever in shackles. Sabbath celebrations were reminders of this. Sabbaths were, each one, holidays of hope. They were sheer grace wrapped in the ribbon of ritual. No wonder Jesus made it His "custom" to honor the Sabbath.

Jesus' first followers took up the same custom, observing the day of rest that God had given at the beginning. Long before Jesus' day, the Hebrew Bible had said that non-Jews as well as Jews would one day keep the Sabbath. Gentile Christians, Paul said later, were like "branches" grafted onto a "rich root," and the root, the heritage of the Jews, was indispensable for the support of the branches. Jesus had just this heritage in mind when He said the Sabbath was made for "humankind." The Jews were the ones who, in telling the Creation story, said the Sabbath was intended for everyone. The Sabbath was a gift offered before there was any ethnic division or any ceremony particular to a specific tribe or nation. And it was in this light that no New Testament writer spoke ill of the Sabbath or dismissed its relevance to Christian life. The day of rest, the seventh day, was welcome and revered.[4]

Adventists acknowledged all this when they took in the Sabbath heritage. And they became the richer for it. Now their hope joined itself to the meeting of human need within the creation God provided. Now their aspiration turned to the making of a people truly whole, and of a world where wholeness would truly thrive.

From the start, Adventists had opposed slavery. By the time of the Civil War, they had embraced nonviolence. Soon, living a healthy life—attending to the whole person, and not least the human body—became a passion. Then the medical work began. Missionaries crossed the sea. Adventist higher education got its start. The church threw itself behind the temperance movement, and defended religious liberty. Ellen White told students they could aspire to "deliberative and legislative councils."[5] The idea of human flourishing was taking hold. In one way and then another and another, Adventists were starting to change the world.

By now, hope colored experience: you lived your days in the light of promise. At the same time, the Sabbath colored hope: you took up the life-affirming perspective of this memorial to Creation and renewal. With each Sabbath came praise and remembrance of God. With each Sabbath came words and deeds of encouragement. Now, believing in the resurrection and return of Christ, you threw yourself into living well on earth. You sought a healthy body, found joy in service and in the sharing of the gospel, and met boredom, malice, and calamity with courage and creative passion.

Work and rest alike made sense. Life on earth was no mere ordeal. It was an opportunity you could seize and savor.

A Journey of Transformation

Or all this *began* to be the case. In truth, the Adventist way is a matter of being and also of becoming: you *are* Adventist, and, with growth, you *become* Adventist. You take up, that is, a journey of transformation, and, as understanding and commitment advance, the practice of hope advances too—it becomes, or may become, more and more authentic.

Many Bible stories picture the life of faith as a journey. From the day Abraham left his hometown, people were always, it seems, on the road. When Jesus began His public ministry, He left His hometown, focusing at first on the villages around the Sea of Galilee, then venturing north and west to Gentile territory and returning from it, and finally heading to Jerusalem, His culture's capital.

In the Gospel of Mark, the "road," or "way," is a key theme, a symbol or picture that shines a light on discipleship. In Mark's account, by the time Jesus was approaching Jerusalem, He and His entourage resembled a 1960s civil rights march. There was a charismatic Leader and His close confidantes, there were edgy authorities, and there were the poor and other vulnerable folk tagging along and hoping desperately for change.

But the disciples still didn't understand, or fully understand, what was going on. According to Mark, they were blind to the essence of Jesus' mission, unable or unwilling to get it.

Finally, the travelers came to Jericho. And as Jesus and "his disciples and a large crowd" were leaving the town, "Bartimaeus . . . , a blind beggar, was sitting by the roadside."[6] The fact that the beggar was blind and in some sense similar to the disciples is crucial, for a transformation was about happen—or better, a journey of transformation. This man was about to become, by contrast with the Twelve, the ideal, or paradigmatic, follower of Jesus.

You can imagine the man's frame of mind as he sat by the roadside. Life had kicked a lot of dust in his face. As for his physical infirmity, it was worse than bad. In that time and place, it symbolized the condemnation of God: people thought the blind were to blame somehow for their blindness, and thought less of them for it. But despite his desolation, Bartimaeus mustered the courage to shout, " 'Jesus, Son of David, have mercy on me!' "

The crowd stiffened, and "many," Mark tells us, ordered the beggar "to be quiet." But Bartimaeus wouldn't have it. He cried out for mercy more loudly than before.

Jesus had heard. He stopped and paid attention. And Bartimaeus "sprang up," the Gospel says, "and came to Jesus." Then, when they asked what he wished for, he simply said, " 'My teacher, let me see again.' "

Jesus complied immediately. But what makes the story profound—spiritually profound—is that Bartimaeus saw Jesus as his *Teacher*. The twelve disciples didn't yet understand, and Mark wants us to interpret the beggar's request in that light. Yes, the blind man yearned to see the sky, the trees, the color of wheat, the curl in a baby's hair. But he also wanted the sight a *teacher* can give: a vision of what can make us better than we are, what can make us whole and help us flourish.

So, on receiving the sight he hoped for, what did Bartimaeus do? For Mark, the answer is the climax of the story: as soon as he could see, Bartimaeus "followed" Jesus "on the road." He began immediately, in other words, to put his new vision—and that means, in part, his new spiritual insight—to good use. Bartimaeus began immediately to take the same path that Jesus did. He determined that he wouldn't drift into self-preoccupation or wasted time or atrocious evil. He would see people and the world through the eyes of Jesus. And by living in such solidarity with Christ, he would grow and flourish and become fully alive.

Years afterward, Paul said that a person who is "baptized" identifies so completely with Jesus as to experience, somehow, both His death and His resurrection. This happens—this burial, this arising from the dead—so that the person "might walk in newness of life." The baptized person begins, like Bartimaeus on the road to Jerusalem, to live "in union with Christ Jesus."[7]

Again and again, the walking metaphor. Again and again, the Christian life as a journey taken in the company of the Great Teacher. When you are the ideal disciple, you are at Jesus' side, engaged in the mission and learning all you can. You practice your hope, and you look always for new insight so you can practice it better. That is how you keep the faith.

You have to imagine Bartimaeus truly blessed and truly joyful. After all, in the Gospel of John, Jesus was remembered as saying that He had entered into His mission so that others "may have life, and have it abundantly." His first followers, so Acts declares, lived "with glad and generous hearts."[8]

It's true that on that road—a road that would pass through Calvary—Bartimaeus was learning to be a man of love. It's true that he was learning to give his cordial consent to the being of others and to make his whole life a bridge over troubled water. No doubt it was a difficult curriculum. But Jesus was a channel of divine grace, and God's biddings are enablings—God gives you strength for the life-altering journey you are called to make.[9]

Paul would one day say, "I worked . . . though it was not I, but the grace of God that is with me." Mark tells the Bartimaeus story in order to evoke a picture of the ideal disciple. It's crucial to remember that this once-blind beggar, now renewed, labored himself, just like Paul. And certainly he himself received, just like Paul, the gift of grace.[10] That gift meant acceptance. It meant deeper understanding. It made Bartimaeus strong to do new and better things. All this was true on day one, and it was true on all the days thereafter.

Being Adventist is like being Bartimaeus. What you *are*—a disciple of Christ—is what you are hoping to *become.* Your faith is a journey, both blessed and joyful, into ever-deeper insight and ever-deeper authenticity.

The Adventist Way Revisited

As we saw in the chapter "Reaching for Radical Hope," Adventists at the beginning made their pledge to Christ and one another in words that were at once simple and practical. Delegates to the 1861 organizing meeting for a "conference" of Michigan congregations shrank from any creedlike statement of belief as a condition of participation. Such a thing, James White argued, would block "new light" and stand in "direct opposition" to the "gifts" of the Holy Spirit. The delegates instead embraced a simple pledge: "We, the undersigned, hereby associate ourselves together as a church, taking the name, Seventh-day Adventists, covenanting together to keep the commandments of God and the faith of Jesus Christ."[11]

The words came from two signature verses of pioneer Adventism, Revelation 12:17 and 14:12, and the words were at once wonderful and fierce: you made that promise, and you had something large to live for; you made that promise, and the crust of self gave way.

But 1861 was near the start of the Adventist journey. The medical work would yet begin. Mission to the world would yet begin. Education and temperance and religious liberty would yet begin. Only later, in other words, would Adventists come to realize the divine call to repair and renew the world. And once these later initiatives had made their beginning, something else would dawn on Adventist members. They would begin to understand that focus on doing what God asks—focus on obedience—can lapse easily into alarm about not being good enough for God, or conceit about being superior to others, or both.

That is why what happened in Minneapolis in 1888 was momentous in Adventist history. The contentious debate at that General Conference meeting strengthened the Adventist sense not only of human inadequacy but also of sheer gratitude for God's acceptance and good favor. Participants saw that "righteousness" is a bounty you receive through faith. Instead of *earning* God's approval, you *welcome* God's grace. You *receive* forgiveness, insight, and strength. In the Christian life, to say it one more way, you benefit from *gifts.*

A passion for human flourishing. The sense that by following Christ you can make a difference. And now, life lived from gratitude instead of fear. All these came to the fore in Adventist thinking after the Michigan meeting of 1861.

A simple declaration made sense when Adventist life was first taking shape. A simple declaration can also be helpful today—perhaps more helpful. Now the whole story of the pioneers—not just the beginning— can be instructive. That whole story suggests a refined yet still uncomplicated summary of Adventist conviction. The pledge we make when we embrace the Adventist way might now be this: *Thanks to the gift of grace, and for the purpose of blessing to all, we join together in keeping the commandments of God and the faith of Jesus.*

Any young person and any new Christian can understand this pledge. Everyone can acknowledge, of course, that growth in Christian life requires further study and fuller explanation. But these few words do express the simple gospel. And they do disclose the heart of Adventism. They say grace, and they say discipleship. In their allusion to signature passages from the book of Revelation, they say "remnant," or courageous few, and they evoke a hope that is both urgent and radical. This pledge articulates a vision as crucial as Sabbath rest and as emancipating as words of forgiveness or the recovery of sight.

A poet spoke of "other spirits" who stand apart "upon the forehead of the age to come" and give the world "another heart, / And other pulses."[12] That, too, is what the Adventist way is about: different hearts and different heartbeats, a counterculture, a style of living that anticipates the age to come—when Christ will reign and evil lose its sway.

Can such a vision for Christian life be too much to bear? Is the demand so high that anyone who embraces it must feel inadequate and weighted down? Once I looked out a window and saw part of the answer.

My older son was eighteen, and my younger son was five. Both boys were in the backyard, with tall trees behind them and the evening sky above. They both had baseball gloves, and they were tossing a tennis ball against the bricks of the house and retrieving the grounders that shot back.

Jonathan, the older one, threw soft-line drives. Jeremy had to throw high-arcing flies just to cover the span, twenty feet or so, to the wall. I began to notice how pleased the two of them were. Separated by so many years, they had never quarreled the way siblings do when they are closer in age. Jonathan was the eager coach, and Jeremy the eager student.

For the younger brother, the demand was high, the distance to his older brother's deftness hard to fathom. But he felt no burden. Certainly there was no harsh code of dos and don'ts between the two of them. They loved each other and knew the younger could flourish when he took his coaching from the older. Jeremy, at five, simply wanted to do his best, and that was exactly what Jonathan was hoping for.

I imagine Bartimaeus in a relationship like that: a disciple eager to learn with a teacher eager to help. I imagine, in other words, that what I saw out the window was an intimation of grace. It was a picture, incomplete yet still revealing, of how a high calling can be lived out in the presence of a truly loving God.

The Christian life takes place, of course, within a circle, or congregation, of other disciples. That circle is a tangible and far from perfect representation of Christ, which makes for complications that we'll explore later in the chapter "The Beloved Community." Still, in God's presence, a high calling inspires and doesn't smother.

All this is liberating. But what might it be, actually *be,* to stand upon the forehead of the age to come? What might it be to live in the manner of the courageous few? That is what we come to next.

---

1. I first heard this story from John Webster of La Sierra University. Later, I met Ginn Fourie. For a telling interpretation of the story by a non-Seventh-day Adventist writer, see John W. DeGruchy, *Reconciliation: Restoring Justice* (London: SCM Press, 2002), 165–170. Jesus' prayer in Luke 23:34.

2. Genesis 1:1 through 2:3; Mark 2:27; Isaiah 58:13.

3. Exodus 20:11 and Deuteronomy 5:15.

4. Isaiah 56:6, 7—a passage Jesus Himself alludes to (in Mark 11:17)—imagines "foreigners" joining themselves to Israel's God; they would one day "keep the sabbath" and worship in "a house of prayer for all peoples." Luke 4:16 notes Jesus' practice; Romans 11:17, 18 contains Paul's perspective. Historians now generally agree that at first, Christians observed the Sabbath of the Hebrew Bible. See, for example, James Carroll, *Constantine's Sword: The Church and the Jews* (Boston: Houghton Mifflin Company, 2001), 145; also consult all of Herold Weiss, *A Day of Gladness: The Sabbath Among Jews and Christians in Antiquity* (Columbia, S.C.: University of South Carolina Press, 2003).

5. From White's *Fundamentals of Christian Education*, 82. This remark is quoted in Jonathan M. Butler, "Adventism and the American Experience," in Edwin S. Gaustad, ed., *The Rise of Adventism* (New York: Harper & Row, 1974), 195.

6. This story takes up verses 46–52 of Mark 10 and can also be found in Matthew 20:29–34 and Luke 18:35–43.

7. See Romans 6:1–4, 11. The phrase from verse 11 appears as in the NEB.

8. John 10:10 and Acts 2:46.

9. Ellen White writes, in *Christ's Object Lessons* (Washington, D.C.: Review and Herald®, 1900), 333, that all God's "biddings are enablings."

10. Paul's testimony appears in 1 Corinthians 15:10.

11. The pledge is cited in *Seventh-day Adventist Encyclopedia*, 310. One account of the meeting, including the discussion of creeds that preceded embrace of the pledge, is in Arthur L. White, *Ellen G. White: The Early Years, 1827–1862* (Washington, D.C.: Review and Herald®, 1985), 453, 454.

12. From "Addressed to Haydon," in John Keats, *Poems*, Everyman's Library Pocket Poets (New York: Knopf, 1994), 12.

5

The Peacemaking Remnant

Have you ever been stifled or stepped on? Ever felt trapped in a job or a relationship? Ever been afraid on the streets? Have you ever fretted over money and bills? Ever wondered if polluted air and water might someday make you sick?

Now imagine being in someone's shoes who is worse off than you. Imagine being so poor you can't feed your family. So unsafe you can't take a walk. So tyrannized you can't speak your mind. Imagine that you have no access to clean water, no protection against thieves and rapists, no hospital or doctor to go to when you or your baby falls sick.

These things make you wince. After all, everyone wants to flourish and be fully alive. We find it distressing if anything gets in the way. So when the prophet Ezekiel spoke words of hope to the exiled people of Israel, he used the word *shalom*—"peace." He did this because in the Hebrew tongue, *shalom* was about food, safety, and freedom; it was about prosperity, well-being, self-respect for the whole community. All this is what people need and want when they feel anxious or think their lives are hanging by a thread. Ezekiel, therefore, thought of God's promise—the Great Promise—as a "covenant of peace."[1] The partnership between God and Israel meant that someday the things that hurt would lose out to the things that heal and restore. Someday, God's people would flourish and be fully alive.

From the start of his Gospel, Luke puts this same peace, this same promise, at the heart of things. He says that just before Jesus' birth, the father of John the Baptist, ecstatic about his own son's arrival, prophesied that God would soon " 'guide our feet into the way of peace.' " Soon afterward, the shepherds heard an angel announcing Jesus' birth and saw "a multitude of the heavenly host" exclaiming, " 'Glory to God in the highest heaven, and on earth peace.' "[2]

Jesus' coming, it turns out, was about peace. The prophets had foretold a day when a new leader would save Israel. Isaiah declared, unforgettably, that this new leader would be the "Prince of Peace." Micah, another prophet, said the new leader—who would come from Bethlehem—would be "the one of peace." Matthew carries the theme of peace from his own version of the birth story, where he makes a point of connecting Jesus to Bethlehem,[3] to the heart of Jesus' spoken ministry, where it is nothing less than the drumbeat you march to. In Matthew 5, he pictures the disciples gathered for training and Jesus telling them that peacemaking will mark their identity as "children of God." Jesus' remarks begin with the Beatitudes, which express God's blessing upon people who cannot in the here and now expect an easy life. But they are the ones who ally themselves, despite difficulty, with the spirit and the way of Jesus. They are humble. They thirst for what is good and true. And their fundamental mission—what they *do*—is peacemaking. "Blessed are the peacemakers," as Jesus says, "for they will be called children of God."[4]

This is not new. The psalmist, sensing that peace is not just a gift but also a vocation, said, "Depart from evil, and do good; seek peace, and pursue it."[5] The prophet Jeremiah even told humiliated Jews to "seek the peace of the city" where they were living as captives. They were to pray to God on behalf of that city because its peace, its "welfare," was the key to their own peace, their own welfare.[6] Even in enemy territory, their vocation was peacemaking.

In calling the disciples to their mission, Jesus was building on the heritage He'd grown up with. How does that heritage, with its promise of peace and its call to peacemaking, link up with the story of the Adventist pioneers? And how does it shed light on the meaning of the Adventist way for today—on what it is, in short, not only to receive but also to *be* a blessing?

Adventism and the Idea of the "Remnant"

Not long after the Great Disappointment of 1844, Adventists embraced the Sabbath and began, every week, to celebrate God's creation and the human work that takes place in it. The hope of the Second Coming had brought them into being in the first place; now their hope began, if only slowly, to connect with earthly yearnings and earthly possibilities. Adventists started to address the same needs and dreams as are encapsulated in the Hebrew word *shalom*. They turned their sights to safety and freedom in human life and began to act on behalf of the aggrieved. Soon health—more precisely, whole-person health, or harmony with God in body, mind, and spirit—attracted their attention. In due course they would even come, these pioneers, to see themselves in roles like that of city mayor or legislative advocate.[7] Adventist concern was widening out, taking in more of those interests and activities that contribute to the overall well-being promised by the covenant of peace.

As Adventism took root, the United States was still supporting slavery, which (to understate the matter) excluded its victims from the domain of peace. Adventists objected. So, in addition to adoption of the seventh-day Sabbath, opposition to slavery made their witness a witness of dissent—of *peacemaking* dissent. The church's pioneers were imperfect, of course, in what they said and did on behalf of peace. Like church members today, they were *becoming* Adventist—learning, that is, how to be what they were called to be. But their witness did hark back to the days before Constantine, the Roman emperor who did so much to cement Christianity into compromise. The Sabbath was their embrace of the church's Jewish roots, despite prejudice against Jews that had hardened under Constantine. Opposition to slavery was their refusal, despite Constantine's vision of church-state solidarity, to equate loyalty to Caesar with loyalty to Christ.

Some Adventists defied the 1850 Fugitive Slave Act by refusing to return runaway slaves. In 1858, Ellen White spoke of the "terrible merchandise" of slavery and deplored the way Christ's "professed followers" were consenting to it with such "heartless indifference." In the same year, Joseph Waggoner wrote in the *Review and Herald* that tolerance of slavery had made the American government a "great idol." By the time of the Civil War, more than fifteen years after 1844, Ellen White was calling slavery a "sin of darkest dye," and Uriah Smith was saying slavery's perpetrators were "dragon-hearted."[8]

Strangely, however, Adventists didn't pursue the security and well-being of the slaves the way the American North did. During the Civil War, they refused, nearly all of them, to bear arms against the South. Some did bring up a "just-war" perspective—one man expressed hope for "a regiment of Sabbath-keepers" who would strike a "staggering blow" to the rebellion of the South—and a few were actually combatants. But Ellen White and other leaders came, in the end, to agreement that participation in war, even this one, violated the Ten Commandments and the teachings of Jesus. When an 1864 change in the U. S. law concerning military conscription allowed members of churches that opposed war to serve in hospitals and take care of freed slaves, Adventism went on record as one of those churches.[9] The pioneers stood for peace but not for violence.

Why? If Jesus asks His followers to be peacemakers—champions of the biblical *shalom*—why not take steps to kill others if necessary in order to deliver people from injustice? There is an answer to this question, and it provides further insight into the church's witness of dissent.

With their embrace of the Sabbath, Adventists had begun interpreting their lives in terms of God's call for a "remnant," a faithful minority who would commit themselves to keeping the commandments of God and the faith of Jesus. The picture of the remnant was enshrined in the book of Revelation, and that book was, for the pioneers, a key source of inspiration. This fact, it turns out, helps us understand why they could work for the well-being of the slaves and yet refuse participation in the Civil War.

John, the author of Revelation, was himself an abused man, exiled from family and friends, suffering from injustice. He knew, and deeply felt, the similar suffering of others, and from this place of pain and deep awareness, he communicated assurance. "Grace to you and peace," he said in chapter 1. In the same chapter, he reported that he had heard the risen Christ say, "Do not be afraid." Later, he described a choir from heaven singing gratitude to Christ: in dying, the voices exclaim, You "ransomed" people—You set them free—so they could live for "God" and "reign on earth."[10]

But it's not just assurance of better prospects for the distressed and the bullied that this book communicates. The "remnant" God delivers is also the "remnant" God galvanizes for "endurance," for full allegiance to the "commandments of God" and the "faith of Jesus."[11] In noticing this, the first Adventists began to believe that they were called to *be* that remnant. To them, Revelation was a book for today, a book for them. They saw their lives in its light.

Jesus' faith was, of course, a Sabbath-keeping faith. What is more, it was a faith in the God—and in the way—of peace. Indeed, when you consider the picture of the "remnant" in the context of Scripture as a whole, the connection with *shalom* is unmistakable. The picture is prominent in the Hebrew Bible as well as the New Testament, and there, especially in the prophets, peace is the heart of the matter. With Israel in exile, Jeremiah reports a promise that God will "gather the remnant" of His "flock" to their own land, where—as when *shalom* prevails—they will enjoy life in a just and safe environment.[12] Later, Zechariah notes God's words to those—the "remnant"—who by this time have returned to Jerusalem: "For there shall be a sowing of peace; the vine shall yield its fruit, the ground shall give its produce, and the skies shall give their dew."[13]

Clearly, those who make up the remnant are recipients of divine favor, destined for the wholeness of life that is peace. But for the prophets, as for the author of Revelation, it is not just divine favor that the remnant receive; it is also responsibility. According to Zechariah, God says, "I will save you, and you shall be a blessing." This echoes what Abraham heard

long before, but now—and very significantly—the prophet offers a surprising vision of *how* blessing will take place. One day an unarmed leader
will appear, riding on the "foal of a donkey." Without military strength,
he will cut off "the chariot from Ephraim and the war horse from Jerusalem." Without coercive force, he will "*command peace* to the nations."[14]

All this was an intimation of Jesus. Hundreds of years later, as His
public mission reached its climax, He rode into Jerusalem on the foal of
a donkey—unarmed but for the persuasive force of a peacemaking mission He hoped would become a movement. After that ride, He shared a
meal (what Christians call the Last Supper) with His followers. He hoped
the broken bread and blood-colored wine—each a symbol of looming
crucifixion, and each shared by everyone—would draw them further into
solidarity with Him and with His mission.

In teaching His followers about the mission, Jesus alluded often to
Ezekiel 34, where talk of the good "shepherd" watching over his "flock"
accompanies the announcement of God's "covenant of peace." Taking
cues from this passage, Jesus addressed His own followers (with due
modesty) as a "little flock." But if they were small, they could still "strive,"
He said, for God's "kingdom." They could still *be* as well as *receive* a
blessing.[15] They could live as the courageous few, and in their loyalty to
the covenant of peace, they could make an impact. Jesus loved peace just
as Ezekiel did. What is more, He aspired to become, by His Father's
grace, the Peacemaker Zechariah had imagined. And by that same grace,
His followers could become peacemakers, too.

Jesus made it clear that peacemaking is an assertive, even a provocative, vocation. In His first sermon, given on Sabbath and recorded in the
Gospel of Luke, Jesus introduced Himself with words from the book of
Isaiah meant to inspire the powerless and to give fair warning to false
leaders and their unjust institutions. God has sent Me, He said, "to bring
good news to the poor. He has sent me to proclaim release to the captives
and recovery of sight to the blind" and "to let the oppressed go free."
When you read the surrounding context in Isaiah, it's plain that the
words Jesus chose evoke the larger theme of peace. "Peace, peace, to the
far and the near, says the LORD" comes just a few lines before what Jesus

quotes, and between the phrases that He quotes comes this line: "I will appoint Peace as your overseer."

The vision was the prophet's; it belonged to the heritage of Israel. Jesus was suggesting that *He* was somehow the fulfillment of the prophecy—that *He* was somehow, this very day, God's Herald, God's Prophet, God's Peacemaker. At first His hearers spoke well of Him. But when He suggested, too, that the promised peace was for Gentiles as well as Jews, they dragged Him out of the synagogue and threatened Him with harm.[16]

This reaction anticipated what would happen to Jesus down the road. It also underscored how inspired words may seem winsome and innocuous—until they call your own biases into question. Prophecy in the abstract offends no one. But when a prophet's words ask *you* to change your mind, they do offend.

When you are a true peacemaker, how do you respond to such offense? How, in general, do you respond to malice and to evil?

Peacemaking Without Violence

On this point, Jesus stood for something truly out of the ordinary. If peacemaking means assertiveness, it turns out to be assertiveness with a difference. As in Zechariah's vision, you forswear the violent bravado of the conventional hero. As in the best-known of Isaiah's servant songs, you bear wounds without recourse to "violence." Though "oppressed" and "afflicted," you pour yourself out even unto "death" so that you can be a healing force and "the will of the LORD" may "prosper."[17]

This comes to classic expression in the Sermon on the Mount. Addressing the disciples in their collective as well as personal witness, Jesus here commended the same generosity as that of the Father, whose sun and rain nourish both the "evil" and the "good." Even though you have heard, " 'An eye for eye and a tooth for a tooth,' " the true peacemaker responds to insult and injury without violence. Even though it's been said, " 'You shall love your neighbor and hate your enemy,' " the true peacemaker marches to a different drumbeat: " 'Love your enemies and pray for those who persecute you.' " Then, in a telling echo of the beatitude on peacemaking, Jesus explained that all this—this unfailing concern, this all-encompassing compassion—is how you "may be children of your Father in heaven."[18]

To many ears, this seems strange. Or better, it seems familiar but unsettling—so unsettling you want to explain it away. Why take it seriously, after all, when Christians long ago welcomed Constantine, the Roman warrior-emperor, into the fold? Why take it seriously when the church itself became a war machine during the Crusades? Why take it seriously when realism demands—as everyone knows—that government authorities prepare at least some of their citizens for killing?

One response is to say that the question is whether or not the wisdom of the world trumps the wisdom of Jesus. The first Adventists read chapter 18 of Revelation, where a voice from heaven says, " 'Fallen, fallen is Babylon the great!' " and another voice chimes in, " 'Come out of her, my people, so that you do not take part in her sins.' " The first Adventists, like the first followers of Jesus, took it for granted that earthbound powers might lead us astray. Paul did insist, in Romans 13, that when you follow Jesus, you respect the governing authorities for the good God intends them to accomplish. But in the same chapter, Paul said, "Owe no one anything, except to love one another. . . . Love does no wrong to a neighbor."[19] So the Christian acknowledges that loyalty to any human institution has limits. Loyalty to Christ is the surpassing loyalty, and for Christians, what "everyone knows" must give way to the deeper vision He announced and lived by.

Another response to the Sermon on the Mount is to say that hope is at the center of all that Jesus says, even when what He says is hard. At the start of the Sermon, He declared that those who embrace the deeper vision may "rejoice and be glad." When you "hunger and thirst for righteousness," when you are "merciful" and "pure in heart," when you persist in peacemaking despite opposition, the path you take leads to God's kingdom.[20] The first great interpretations of Jesus likewise centered on hope. The crux of Revelation, for example, is that the way of Christ is the way that wins. One of the great interpreters of the Radical Reformation says the "point" of the visionary writing you find in this book is "that people who bear crosses are working with the grain of the universe."[21] *With* the grain, not against it. In other words, when you love radically, you are headed in the best possible direction, the direction that, in God's creation and from God's perspective, is *most natural.* Greed and violence go *against* the grain—rub against reality, and come, in the end, to everlasting doom. Love abides forever.

There is still another response to the "strangeness" of what Jesus says. It is to say *how* the peacemaking He envisioned actually helps. How, for example, does a witness who pursues freedom for slaves yet refuses to bear arms against the South make a real difference? If you stand for peace but not for violence—not even for "good" violence—what keeps you from irrelevance?

How Peacemaking Helps

In one way, of course, the answer is as simple as two plus two. Standing for peace is about a whole range of *positive* commitments. *Shalom* means food, safety, and freedom, and it means prosperity, well-being, and self-respect—for everyone. So you are a peacemaker when you grow wheat or repair cars or design computers; when you build a business or run a hospital; when you make music or plant gardens or paint pictures; when you love your spouse or become a mentor to a child.

But for all the ordinariness of the peacemaking vocation, it is also extraordinary. Peacemakers run afoul of conventional wisdom. They embrace and teach the gospel—the provocative announcement of God's will and way that, from day one, made Jesus controversial. And in that light, they stand apart. As others become comfortable with the suffering of others or make it worse for their own benefit, peacemakers mourn the sufferer's plight and seek to amend it. To this end, they take risks. The best of them take dangerous risks.

The best Adventists have taken risks. As we have seen, when the 1850 Fugitive Slave Act required Americans in the North to assist in returning escaped slaves to their owners, Ellen White counseled Adventists to disobey—and she wrote, "We must abide the consequences of violating this law."[22]

Mary Britton was an Adventist who in 1902 became the first African American licensed to practice medicine in Kentucky. Through her speaking and writing, she spent a lifetime fighting segregation and standing for women's suffrage. Her speeches and newspaper articles were luminous and hopeful. She inspired Paul Laurence Dunbar to write a poem in her honor—as one whose "fearless voice and strong . . . / Roused justice from her sleep."[23]

Somewhat later, in South America, Manuel Camacho and American missionaries Ana and Fernando Stahl teamed up to strengthen the Adventist presence in the Peruvian highlands. Over 90 percent of the populace there was under the thumb of the 10 percent in the landowners' circle, and Camacho wrote, "The only sure way of salvation from the subjugation in which we find ourselves is learning to read." Reading would open eyes, and the exploited would realize their exploitation. So, besides preaching the gospel and attending to illness, Camacho and the Stahls established schools. This inflamed the landowner press and brought threats and mob attacks against these Adventists. But even when it was dangerous to do so, they persisted in addressing the need—the whole-person need—they saw around them.[24]

We saw in an earlier chapter that during the Nazi period, a courageous Adventist named John Weidner defied the authorities. He helped organize a network to spirit Jews away to safety. One of his partners was his sister, and the Nazis killed her. The United States, Britain, the Netherlands, France, Belgium, and Israel all honored him for what he did.[25]

At about the same time and with similar defiance, Irene Morgan, then twenty-seven years old and recovering from surgery, boarded a bus in Virginia that was bound for her home in Baltimore. On that trip, this Adventist woman refused to surrender her seat to a white couple when the insolent driver demanded it, and she was arrested for breaking segregation laws. Thurgood Marshall, who later became a Supreme Court justice, defended her, and the result was a landmark Supreme Court decision declaring segregation in interstate travel to be unconstitutional. What she did in 1944, eleven years before Rosa Parks, inspired the idea of the "freedom ride," which would become a staple of the American civil rights movement. In 2001, Irene Morgan received the Presidential Citizens Medal for her courage and tenacity. She "took the first step," the citation said, "on a journey that would change America forever."[26]

So far, it's easy to see how peacemaking, even risky peacemaking, helps. But again, if Christians uphold the faith of Jesus to the point of refusing violence, how, when violence seems necessary, can they truly make a difference?

That question is more difficult to answer. Except for long ago, during the centuries closest to the Resurrection, most Christians agreed to play down what Jesus said, or even to explain it away. It became conventional, for example, for churches to declare loyalty to the army of their nation, even if that meant church members were slaughtering other church members. Christians forgot that the gospel of Jesus transcends ethnicity and empire.

Still, in each era, some resisted this drift from the original vision. Some kept on stepping to a drumbeat that was out of the ordinary, kept on making peace in an unconventional way. Without apology or embarrassment they embraced the love that reaches out to foe and friend alike and makes its point without descending into violence. How can this be so? What justifies it?

It will help if you first of all imagine an enemy who is resorting, where you live, to suicide bombings. Your society—customers in your restaurants, commuters on your buses—are dying. Now ask if you would argue for a tit-for-tat response. Would you call for a build up of suicide bombers on *your* side of the conflict? Would you encourage *your* friends and children to become suicide bombers themselves?

I suppose not. But you *could* be that sort of person. You could be ready to pay this—or pay any—moral price in order to defend yourself or your society. Then, if it seemed like something you had to do, you might even hold babies hostage, or torture pregnant women, or force ten-year-olds to go to war.

Not a chance; that's not you.

Of course it's not, and here is the point: once you acknowledge *any* limits to the evil you would do in order to fend off harm, you have to allow that the way of Jesus may make sense. Moral limits, after all, prevent downward moral spirals in which, to protect themselves, people keep outbidding their enemies in the belligerence of their responses to attacks or potential attacks, and their enemies do the same. Otherwise, violence only grows more and more horrific.

The fact is that when people say, "If you hurt or threaten us, we'll do anything it takes to stop you," the result is disastrous. But moral limits do help. And when people combine moral limits with moral aspiration, they open up the possibility of human transformation.

In the Sermon on the Mount, Jesus said His followers would be "the light of the world." Shining like a city "on a hill," they would draw others into the praise of God and so help God's will to be done "on earth as it is in heaven."[27] They would be exemplary, and by that means they would be transformative.

In Jesus' vision—Jesus' take on the heritage of Israel—moral limits govern peacemaking. You refuse to cross the border into violence and hate. You pursue your neighbor's well-being, even when your neighbor's armies have forced you to live in a city not your own. You pray even for your persecutors.

When a society says No to suicide bombing, it puts the brakes on moral decay. When Jesus forbade a violent response to evil, He did the same. When He embodied true love of enemies, He planted the flag for a higher moral vision and opened a door to human transformation.

God works out the divine purpose, said one New Testament scholar, "through a 'remnant,' a minority ready to think and act ahead of the community as a whole, and so keep alive the vision of God's redemptive way."[28] That's what peacemakers who transcend ethnicity and empire are *for*. In a world of narrow loyalties and persistent conflict, they keep before the human race the vision of God's redemptive way—the way made manifest through Jesus.

At the start of chapter 2, we saw how an Adventist congregation in Sarajevo responded to conflict among Serbs, Croats, and Muslims in Bosnia. Members teamed up with the Adventist Development and Relief Agency to organize an informal postal service that somehow transcended religious and ethnic discord. Working in concert, Serb, Croat, and Muslim volunteers began to deliver truckloads of letters and packages past the Serb-controlled outskirts of the city into the most isolated sectors of Sarajevo. The whole operation depended on the cooperation and goodwill of the warring factions.

Explaining this to a newspaper reporter, Milan Suslic, an Adventist pastor and relief agency director, said "one bullet in a convoy" would ruin their initiative. When the reporter wondered how Adventists could sustain the necessary cooperation and goodwill, he stressed that they were "not part of any nationality or any side in the war." In words that epitomize the gospel of peace, the pastor declared, "We are nobody's and everybody's."

Members of this tiny Sarajevo congregation had scaled a summit of moral aspiration few others even attempt. They could see past religious and ethnic discord to the immeasurable Yes of divine generosity and restraint. In their corner of God's world, they were a remnant who thought and acted ahead of the community around them. They were keeping alive, in a place otherwise besieged by darkness, the vision of God's redemptive way.

We turn now from the *life* of Christ's followers to the crucial *teachings* that undergird that life. In further exploring Adventism's core convictions, we'll see further support for the mission of peacemaking. But at the end of all this exploration, the peacemaking mission—its leader, its goals, its methods—will seem like something of a gamble. Nothing removes *all* doubt.

However, indifference to the human prospect makes no sense. And as for fixing things by belligerence—that seems, at best, doubtful. In *Fiddler on the Roof,* Tevye is a Jewish father who lives with his family in a browbeaten Eastern European village. Jews have been ordered to leave within three days. Ethnic and religious malice hangs over everything. From Tevye's anxious friends comes the suggestion to put up a fight—"an eye for an eye," one of them exclaims, "and a tooth for a tooth." Tevye replies, "Very good. And that way the whole world will be blind and toothless."

But maybe the whole world will come to something better. Hope for something better is what keeps the faithful standing tall, and hope is what we turn to now.

---

1. On this, see Ezekiel 34:25–31.

2. Luke 1:79; 2:13, 14.

3. Matthew 2:6 quotes Micah 5:2, where the context (see Micah 5:5) makes clear that the One to come forth from Bethlehem will be the "one of peace." The "Prince of Peace" reference is in Isaiah 9:6.

4. Matthew 5:9. I rely on Willard M. Swartley, *Covenant of Peace* (Grand Rapids, Mich.: Eerdmans, 2006), 53f.

5. Psalm 34:14.

6. Jeremiah 29:7. I quote, initially, from the KJV; "welfare" is how, in this verse, the NRSV translates *shalom.*

7. On all this, see chapter 2.

8. The first Ellen White quote is from *Spiritual Gifts,* vol. 1 (Battle Creek, Mich.: James White, 1858, published, in a facsimile reproduction, in Washington, D.C., by the Review and Herald® in 1945), 191. The next three quotes—the first from Joseph Waggoner, the second from Ellen White, and the third from Uriah Smith—are cited in Douglas Morgan, *Adventism and the American Republic* (Knoxville: University of Tennessee Press, 2001), 26–29.

9. The "regiment" quote is from Joseph Clark, "The War! The War!!" *Review and Herald,* 23 September 1862, 134. On the church and military conscription, see Douglas Morgan, "The Beginnings of a Peace Church: Eschatology, Ethics and Expedience in Seventh-day Adventist Responses to the Civil War," *Andrews University Seminary Studies* 45 (2007): 38, 39.

10. Revelation 1:4, 17; 5:9, 10.

11. Consider Revelation 12:17 and 14:12—signature passages for Adventist faith.

12. See Jeremiah 23:3–8; for Jeremiah's conception of *shalom,* see, e.g., 29:5–7 and, especially, 33:6–9.

13. Zechariah 8:12, 13.

14. Zechariah 8:12, 13; 9:9, 10; cf., e.g., Matthew 21:1–11.

15. Luke 12:31, 32.

16. Luke 4:18, 19 records Jesus' vision, taken from Isaiah 61:1, 2 and 58:6. The peace references occur in Isaiah 57:19 and 60:17. For the reaction to Jesus, read on, in Luke 4, to verse 30.

17. These ideas (and quoted words) are from Isaiah 53.

18. See Matthew 5:38–45.

19. From Revelation 18, see verses 2 and 4. In Romans 13; cf. verses 8–10 with verses 1–3 of Romans 13.

20. From the Beatitudes, in Matthew 5:3–12.

21. From John Howard Yoder's essay, "Patience as Method in Moral Reasoning: Is an Ethic of Discipleship Absolute?" The essay is quoted in Stanley Hauerwas, *With the Grain of the Universe* (Grand Rapids. Mich.: Brazos Press, 2001), 17.

22. Ellen White, *Testimonies for the Church,* 1:201, 202, cited in Douglas Morgan, *Adventism and the American Republic,* 29.

23. I first learned of Mary Britton from Doug Morgan. For the information here, see "Great Black Kentuckians," Kentucky Commission on Human Rights, http://kchr.ky .gov/about/gallergreatblack.htm?&pageOrder=0&selectedPic=36; "Historical Highlights of the Lima Drive Seventh-day Adventist Church 1894–2004," found at http://www .scc-adventist.org/forms/Lexington%20Timeline%20History.pdf; and, for the poem, "Britton, Mary E.," found at http://www.astr.ua.edu/4000WS/BRITTONM .html. All sites accessed October 25, 2008.

24. See Charles Teel Jr., "The Radical Roots of Peruvian Adventism," *Spectrum* 21 (December 1990): 5–18.

25. See Gay Block and Malka Drucker, *Rescuers: Portraits of Moral Courage in the Holocaust* (New York: TV Books, 1998), 80–85; and the 1994 obituary, "John Weidner, 81, Who Foiled Nazis," *New York Times* http://query.nytimes.com/gst/fullpage .html?res=9D05E0DA1E38F937A15756C0A962958260. Site accessed on November 2, 2008.

26. Carol Morello, "The Freedom Fighter a Nation Nearly Forgot," *Adventist Review,* February 1, 2001, 8–11. I also consulted http://www.nytimes.com /2007/08/13/us/ 13kirkaldy.html. Site accessed October 25, 2008.

27. See Matthew 5:14–16. For the last phrase, from the Lord's Prayer, see Matthew 6:10.

28. G. H. C. Macgregor, *The New Testament Basis of Pacifism* (New York: Fellowship of Reconciliation, 1936), 82, 83.

6

Pictures of the Kingdom Coming

Look at the stars, and you feel small. Consider fear and sorrow in the human heart, and you know you're vulnerable. Look inward with an honest eye, and you see your flaws. Now put the grip of circumstance into the picture, and you may slump into discouragement, or even hopelessness.

The playwright Tennessee Williams has one of his characters reply irritably to his mother's "Rise an' shine" wake-up call. "I'll rise—but I won't shine." He's too anxious—too sullen and resentful—to chase the dark away.[1]

Anyone can feel this way. Still, people with distressed and battered hearts sometimes muster courage to dispel the darkness—to shine as well as rise—and they become beacons to the stormed-tossed souls around them. One of these was Ruby Bridges, the six-year-old who, starting in November of 1960, walked into school every day through a mob of hecklers.

White citizens of New Orleans hated Ruby Bridges for being the first black child to enter that city's long-segregated public schools. Accompanied by federal marshals, she had to bear, twice every day, threats and catcalls from the glowering throng that lined the way to and from her school. And while she was inside, she found the hallways and classrooms empty. White families were conducting a boycott.

Ruby Bridges's teachers began to wonder when she would fold under the abuse. But this little six-year-old persisted for months, a tiny, astonishing pioneer of American civil rights.

A Harvard psychiatrist who studied children in crisis was drawn to her epic battle and came to know her. At first he believed she was denying her anxieties. He thought she would crumple. Then he noticed that she was smiling back at those who scorned her. He learned, too, that every night she was praying for them, and that she was keeping in her mind the prayer Jesus uttered while He was on the cross for the forgiveness of His executioners. Her strength, the psychiatrist could see, was like the sun.

It turned out that Ruby's family, minister, and church friends were coaching and encouraging her shining witness, and their efforts had taken hold and were keeping her strong. Once, in a potent revelation, Ruby told her psychiatrist friend that God knew what was happening and might not "rush" to do anything, "not right away." But this was no reason to stop what she was doing. She was convinced, she said, that "there will come a day, like you hear in church."[2]

Her words were wings against the pull of hate and hopelessness. *There will come a day.* Ruby Bridges believed the message of hope that you hear in church, and she felt no paralyzing fear. She was small and susceptible to harm. Her circumstances were painful and bewildering. But instead of being self-absorbed and beaten down, she embraced the promises of God. She was *living* the adventure of hope.

Becoming Adventist

The disciples of Jesus heard their risen Lord say that they would be shining witnesses, in Jerusalem first and finally to the ends of the earth. Days before, while Jesus was in the tomb, ruined dreams had left them desolate and broken. Now their Leader's presence was like the rainbow, an arc of hope across a brightening sky. After Jesus had renewed their confidence and divulged their mission, the disciples saw a "cloud" lift Him "out of their sight." Then, while they were still "gazing" upward, "two men in white robes" came with words of reassurance: "This Jesus, who has been taken up from you into heaven, will come in the same way as you saw him go into heaven."[3]

Thus, according to Luke, did the disciples become *Adventists,* or believers in the "blessed hope" of the Second Coming, the Second Advent.[4] On the way to Jerusalem and crucifixion, Jesus had predicted the return of " 'the Son of Man coming in a cloud' with power and great glory." Now, galvanized by the resurrection and newly reassured, the disciples began to believe that Jesus was this Son of man, and that He would be the One to return.[5]

They were still living between their dreams and disappointments, as everyone does. But now they had in their minds a picture of the kingdom coming, of the day when Jesus would upend the evil powers and the peace of God would fill the earth. It was just a picture, but it was as vivid as green grass shining after rain. The ascension of Jesus, and the words of hope that followed, had pierced the boundaries of the ordinary. Like Moses at the burning bush, they had felt the presence of holiness. Now, trembling with wonder, they felt themselves newly robust, trusting, and determined.

This and other pictures of the kingdom coming would enable the disciples to live the adventure of hope. Through high times and low, they would stand tall. They would share their confidence with others, and their confidence would come to shape the church's story and its way of life. Down the years it would help make courage like that of Ruby Bridges possible.

There will come a day. If that conviction was a defining feature of early Christian faith, it was also a defining feature—at first *the* defining feature— of early Adventism. The movement's pioneers savored in particular the vivid pictures and tumultuous drama of Daniel and Revelation. The earliest of them followed the interpretation of William Miller and thought they knew the very date of the Second Coming. But Jesus didn't appear on October 22, 1844, and their confidence was blasted. They tasted a sorrow so bitter it is still remembered as the Great Disappointment.

From the start, then, Adventists realized that even a people of great hope must, as one writer said later, bear "shattered dreams" and contend with "the silence of God." Pioneer Adventists had ventured forth, as James White remarked at the time, in "the blazing light" of prophecies they thought they fully comprehended. But now, with "disappointed hopes and stricken hearts," they had to find a deeper faith.[6]

Many, in fact, lost their faith. But the resilient held on, and their confidence matured as they recovered from the Great Disappointment and began the rich experience of Sabbath observance. As time passed, the Sabbath was a regular reminder of Christianity's Jewish heritage, with its passion for generosity in the here and now. More and more, as we saw in chapter 1, Adventists set their focus on the *practice* of hope— the shape of life and character when you live by the light of the returning Christ.

Hope Transforming Life

One of the best of twentieth-century philosophers was Ludwig Wittgenstein, an Austrian of Jewish descent. He sympathized with the biblical vision, including Christianity, and he was convinced that practice— the daily living out of what you believe—is the point of religious faith. As for the Bible's pictures of the future, he believed their influence was immense. Such pictures, once grasped, are, he declared, "enough to make me change my whole life."[7]

That is certainly the ideal in Scripture itself. According to Matthew's Gospel, Jesus said that on the day "the Son of Man comes in his glory," He will "sit on the throne of his glory" to pass judgment on all people. This is another picture of the kingdom coming, and here, hope's connection to how we live in the present is as plain as daylight. The message is that when Jesus returns in glory, He will have a decisive question for everyone: have you been compassionate?

In the end, the Son of man will give His blessing to those who have fed, welcomed, and cared for the vulnerable, down to the "least" of them. What matters most, according to this picture of the kingdom coming, is whether you embody the Christlike mercy that is both mindful of human need and active to meet that need.

The Son of man will even declare that how you treated others is how you treated Him. He will say that when you cared, you "did it to me," and when you withheld care, you withheld it from "me."[8] He so identifies with human beings that He feels what they feel—He regards their lot as somehow His. According to this picture, when we meet others, we meet Christ.

Thus the future has *present* relevance—it colors my life right now. The Jesus I will see on the coming day is addressing me now, and I must live now as everyone will live once He has returned in triumph.

In yet another picture, Jesus said the kingdom coming is like a man who, just before leaving on a journey, entrusted money to people who were working for him. When he returned, he praised those who had used their money to make a profit. But he rebuked the man who was "afraid" and hid his money instead of investing it. Again, this is a picture, and it says that while you are waiting for the Son of man's return, you set out to make a difference. You try to change things for the better.[9]

The world's "a mighty cruel place," an old Broadway musical declares. But there's "something still of good" in it, and so we "work and strive while we're alive" to find a better way.[10] In Jesus' picture, just this is what the owner expects of those he entrusts with money. In true discipleship, you refuse immobilizing fear. You invest your gifts. You let your dreams and not your worries shape the day.

It's not that the Bible denies how difficult life is. We have been considering words from Matthew 25. Just before this, in chapter 24, Jesus offers a series of harrowing predictions: before His final triumph there will be wars and rumors of wars, betrayals and lawlessness, forced flights and shameless deceptions. The Son of man will interrupt these troubles with His appearance in "glory," but no one will know the day or hour. So lives will unfold—*do* unfold—in the midst of difficulty. The key, Jesus says, is staying "awake" and remaining "at work."[11]

The pagan culture dominant at the time of the first Christians saw neither goodness nor grace in human history. For Greeks and Romans alike, turbulence and upheaval in life were inevitable, senseless, terrifying. Dreams deferred or shattered had left them thinking the material world—all you touch and smell and see—was somehow second-rate, more like a prison than a home. They didn't believe things earthy are good, or as God says in Genesis 1, "very good."[12]

Jesus' confidence that all things material come from God made Him forward-looking even in the midst of turbulence and upheaval. He had hope, and it was a hope grand and daring enough to motivate adventurous action today. You aren't tethered like an ox to a cart or a slave to a master. With the freedom God gives, you can make your mark on a world that is still in the making. It's your job—and your joy—to invest in the future.

Dreams of Hard-won Victory

The theme of struggle capped by victory suffuses other parts of Scripture that announce hope through vivid pictures and tumultuous drama. As Adventists often say, this struggle is "the great controversy," the battle of good with evil, the conflict between Christ and Satan.[13] For insight into that controversy, two key documents are Daniel and Revelation. Both books offer an "apocalyptic" point of view. In other words, both express the kind of visionary thinking that confronts crisis through poetic images that grab you by the throat. When you pay attention, you end up with a fresh and startling perspective. Writing that inspires such perspective has always been important for Adventists, and both these books continue to shape Adventist consciousness.

Daniel is both a story of moral heroism and a promise of deliverance from evil. We'll return to it in a later chapter. For now, what matters about the book is that an evil empire has exiled the Israelites from home, and they are wedged under the thumb of tyrants. In the face of this, the story of Daniel, with all its intrigues and audacity, conveys both moral passion and defiant hope. The dreams Daniel interprets, with their weird statues and mesmerizing animals, articulate the coming and going of imperial power and the triumph at last of the kingdom of God. In these ways, the book presents a vision meant to fortify and encourage an afflicted people. That, of course, is the point of visionary poetry and prose in Scripture: to fortify and to encourage.

77

Revelation is similar to Daniel. It brings the whole Bible to a compelling, if often enigmatic, climax. It is the account of a dream that is at once hideous and beautiful: it disturbs and it consoles. The author is John. He has offended the Roman authorities, and from his place of exile he writes words that bristle with all things sinister and evil yet give voice to a hope that gleams like fire. Neither a chronicle of doomsday nor a fantasy of easy life, the book foretells a victory—both final and hard-won—for Christ and all who follow Christ.

From the start, the author communicates confidence: "Grace to you and peace," he says. Then he assures readers that his message comes from Jesus Christ, now risen from the dead, and now, despite Roman emperors, the "ruler of the kings of the earth."[14] Astonishing words and pictures cascade onto every page and from beginning to end press home encouragement that helps you face the facts—and then face forward. "Do not be afraid," Jesus says at the book's beginning. When you worship God, you are "blessed," He says at the end.[15]

Even under Caesar's frown, even under his spurious peace and terrible contempt for human dignity, John gives voice to praise. In chapters 4–7, a series of hymns—freedom songs, you might call them—celebrates God and the potential that God sees in the world. God is "worthy," says one of these songs, because God "created all things." No past or present power, nor any that looms ahead, has the capacity to frustrate the divine will forever. What is more, the Creator identifies with Jesus, "the Lion of the tribe of Judah" who by His death liberated people so they could be a blessing themselves.[16] This means the Creator is as generous as Jesus was and intends the same good things for human beings, the same redemption from evil, the same satisfying mission.

I saw my brother once as he was near the end of basic training as an army medic. This was during the Vietnam War, before military service in America was all volunteer, and he had been drafted out of law school. He had managed to get the weekend off for my wedding, and he wanted everyone to know how impossible it was to have a life while the drill sergeants had such complete control. He and the others weren't long in the barracks, he said, until cynicism set in. If someone asked whether your feet were blistered, you said, "It doesn't matter." If someone asked whether you thought the food would be better tomorrow, you said the same thing. "It doesn't matter" was a byword—a phrase you repeated over and over because you felt so stuck. The only hope you had was for an end to basic training. Until then, nothing you did or said could make a difference.

For those few weeks, the young men in basic training felt like the purveyors of pessimism so common in cultures untouched by biblical hope. Marcus Aurelius, who was both an emperor of Rome and a distinguished philosopher, believed all things move in circles. "Everything now is just as it was in the time of those whom we have buried," he declared. In this he echoed Aristotle, the Greek philosopher, and their perspectives are reflected in those of many others over multiple cultures who have seen no prospect for real change on earth.[17]

Revelation, on the other hand, harks back to the Hebrew idea of Creation, with its premise of a good God making a good world for people who can have creative impact themselves. Human beings reflect God's "image"—they can add their own touches to what God has done; they can write music, build bridges, stage festivals, devise governments.[18] When you live inside a worldview like that, you can't think of life as a treadmill that takes you nowhere. Life is an opportunity, and you can be a blessing. What is more, you don't give in when a bad turn tempts you to think that nothing you do can really matter.

True Christian hope is never passive, as if you were at some grimy bus stop where nothing happens and all you can do is wait for a ride to somewhere else. Hope is active, always looking to make an impact. In the Bible, that's what having God as our Maker means.

To catch the import, imagine the man in Jesus' story who hid his money rather than invest it. Had he lived by the vision I've just described, he could have set his sights on larger goals. Words like the ones in Revelation's freedom songs are meant, after all, to set you free from immobilizing fear.

Toward the end of chapter 7, John depicts a scene of rapturous joy, with God enthroned, the risen Lamb beside Him, and worshipers are all around. They have come out of "the great ordeal"—if John imagines the way to permanent peace, he also acknowledges the setbacks, the atrocities, the terror. But *there will come a day, like you hear in church,* and now these worshipers are singing their praise of God and celebrating a world fully transformed, a humanity with its tears wiped away.[19]

From here, the poetry rolls on like thunder. Now six angels, all with trumpets, sound new notes of alarm, followed by a seventh angel trumpeting news that the kingdom of this world has become the kingdom of God. Again in chapters 8–11, hope has its eyes open to the way the world really is, and again, hope finds fulfillment.

Next a zoo of monsters, full of brutal deeds and crooked words, make war on the Messiah and on those who "keep the commandments of God and hold fast to the faith of Jesus."[20] Yet chapters 12–14 again bring assurance for the faithful—assurance that confederates of evil meet their doom, and opponents of evil find fulfillment. When you follow Christ, you are working with, not against, the grain of the universe. Despite appearances, all things are headed in the direction of grace, of peace and blessedness. It is the business of apocalyptic writing to make that point.[21]

The basic theme—*in great difficulty, great confidence*—repeats itself again in chapters 15–18. Then, with Revelation's climactic ending in chapters 19–22, comes the final defeat of evil power, and along with that the resurrection of evil's victims, the renewal of creation, the city of God come down to earth, its radiance like jasper, its river bright as crystal, its bounty overflowing, its peace and praise a sweet and everlasting melody.[22]

Thus the writer's inspired imagination conjures up a day of unshadowed beauty and perfect joy. To get there, you follow the Lamb. You let His spirit and His dreams, His realism and adventure, His joy, His wide-reaching love, and His unfettered hope shape your spirit and your dreams. You stand tall against every false wish, every desire to hoard God's gifts or escape responsibility or pay no heed to truth.

And all the while, you are blessed.[23]

A New World on Its Way

Like the sculptor who sees a lion in a block of stone, those who know the pictures of the kingdom coming see a new world on its way. Seeing that world, they engage in the life of their own time, straining "in the mud and the muck," as a poet of today has written, "to move things forward."[24] They find hardship along the way, but also many satisfactions: "The hill of Zion yields / A thousand sacred sweets, / Before we reach the heavenly fields, / Or walk the golden streets."[25] Life on earth is no meaningless parenthesis, no prison of dark routine.

Still, the journey is turbulent. During the nineteenth century, the worldly wise, tired of religion and increasingly self-assured, were confident in upward evolution: they saw steady progress toward perfection. But the twentieth century, with all its greed and war and terror, brought that vision, that starry-eyed optimism, down like a rock. Nor has the twenty-first century revived it. Now the worldly wise imagine a gloomier prospect, a long and graceless evolution toward . . . nothingness.

But when you embrace the Advent hope, the turbulence, however hard to bear, doesn't crush your confidence. You face the facts and still face forward.

Little is predictable in life, and much is startling: setbacks weave in and out of breakthroughs. Only from long distance, it seems, can you see God's victory taking shape. Or maybe God alone can see that far—the world, after all, is so many-sided and complex, our hearts so prone to ups and downs, our eyesight so limited and skewed.

But faith sees light when light spills through the breaks in the clouds. Once kings or dictators told you how to live. Once the highest human goal was military domination. Once slaves, women, and the poor had hardly any voice or any life. Now, with the biblical vision spread far, people responsive to that vision are more numerous, and agreement that compassion outshines unbridled power is wider than before. Now tyranny, greed, and violence meet not only human cries but also human censure. Signs of transformation do appear, even if those appearances take us by surprise.

Yet the gains, it is true, are frail as paper. Neglect and violence persist, and both the weapons humanity devises and the people who use these weapons grow ever more alarming. What is more, disparity of wealth and opportunity remains, or worsens, and the vast refuse of prosperity puts the environment at risk. Even the most advantaged, meanwhile, still struggle to be good, or even to feel good.

So is the world better than it used to be? In some ways it is; in some ways it certainly is not. If men and women can make a difference for the better, they can also make a difference for the worse.

The Advent hope says simply this: Christ's resurrection, seen against the backdrop of divine creation, means that we can, by God's grace, make a better world. It certifies, moreover, that though the struggle between good and evil continues to rage, a new day will come nevertheless. The victory of the Lamb gives us strength to face deep difficulty with deep confidence.

The Advent hope also says this: The world is bountiful and dangerous alike, and you have to stay alert as you stay on the job. You can't know the day or hour when the next monster will arise, or the next hero; when the next prophet will face an iron fist, or, by some miracle, strike down a long-lived prejudice; when the next trumpet will sound a note of alarm or a fanfare of joy.

So you embrace what Martin Luther King called "the fierce urgency of now." You keep an eye out for unbridled power and bear witness against it. You watch for unexpected opportunity and goodness and make investments in the future. You stay ready always—ready this moment—to follow Jesus.[26]

Each day those who live by God's grace not only rise but also shine, for, as the prophet declared, God's "light has come, and the glory of the LORD has risen upon you." You do what you can to scatter the darkness.[27] Like Ruby Bridges, you believe, even in the face of threats and catcalls, that *there will come a day, like you hear in church.*

The Blind Boys of Alabama, the gospel music group, have it right. They sing a song that says in part: "Jesus gonna be here, gonna be here soon. / I'm gonna leave this place better than the way I found it was. /

Jesus gonna be here, gonna be here soon." That is surely the point. Pictures of the kingdom coming fortify mind and heart alike. Against all blinkered vision and every looming horror, the "blessed hope" alerts the eye to possibilities as well as problems.

The persistence of evil is a fact, and easy optimism a snare and a delusion. But when you are Adventist, your dreams and not your worries shape the day.

---

1. Tennessee Williams, *The Glass Menagerie* (New York: New Directions Books, 1966), 46.

2. See Robert Coles, *The Moral Life of Children* (Boston: Atlantic Monthly Press, 1986), 22–25; and Robert Coles, "The Inexplicable Prayers of Ruby Bridges," *Christianity Today,* August 9, 1985, 17–20.

3. Acts 1:9–11.

4. The phrase "blessed hope," much loved in Adventism, is from Titus 2:13.

5. Luke 21:27 is Jesus' prediction in Jerusalem. Compare Acts 7:54–56, in which Stephen identified Jesus with the Son of man.

6. The quoted phrases are from Janice Daffern, "Singing in a Strange Land," in *Pilgrimage of Hope,* Roy Branson, ed. (Takoma Park, Md.: Association of Adventist Forums, 1986), 91, 96. The James White quotation is also from her essay, 94.

7. The quotations are from Wittgenstein's *Lectures and Conversation on Aesthetics, Psychology, and Religious Belief,* B. Cyril, ed. (Berkeley: University of California Press, 1967), 53, 57, and are cited in James Wm. McClendon Jr., *Doctrines: Systematic Theology,* vol. 2 (Nashville: Abingdon, 2002), 77. In McClendon's *Witness: Systematic Theology,* vol. 3 (Nashville: Abingdon, 2000), the author discusses Wittgenstein's biography, in his chapter 6, pages 227–270.

8. See Matthew 25:31–46.

9. See Matthew 25:14–30.

10. From "Johnny's Song," performed by the peace-loving toy maker in Paul Green's and Kurt Weill's *Johnny Johnson,* first produced in 1936.

11. Matthew 24; the quoted words are from verses 30, 42, and 46 and make points repeated in chapter 25.

12. Genesis 1:31.

13. This was a key theme for Ellen White and is famous from her book *The Great Controversy* (Mountain View, Calif.: Pacific Press®, 1911).

14. Revelation 1:4, 5.

15. Revelation 1:17 and 22:7–9.

16. Revelation 4:11 and 5:5, 9, 10.

17. The quotation, from Marcus's *Meditations,* is cited in Langdon Gilkey, *Maker of Heaven and Earth* (New York: Doubleday & Company, 1965), 297.

18. On "image of God," see Genesis 1:26, 27.

19. See chapters 4–7.

20. Chapter 14:12. This is a signature text for Adventist life and practice.

21. Stanley Hauerwas takes a book title from John Howard Yoder's remark that the "point" of apocalyptic is that "people who bear crosses are working with the grain of the universe," quoting him in *With the Grain of the Universe* (Grand Rapids, Mich.: Brazos Press, 2001), 17.

22. Chapters 19–22.

23. " 'Blessed is the one who keeps the words of the prophecy,' " says Revelation 22:7.

24. These words are from Marge Piercy's poem, "To be of use," found, among other places, in Garrison Keillor's collection of *Good Poems* (New York: Viking, 2002), 157.

25. From the familiar hymn "Marching to Zion."

26. The King phrase is from the "I Have a Dream" speech, available in numerous anthologies.

27. From Isaiah 60:1.

7

Pain and Promise

Watch the news, read the paper, consult your own life story: from casualties of war and deadly weather to lost loves and lost health and dreams that don't come true, pain is everywhere.

It explodes fiercely. Or it comes on as silently as cats' feet. It leaves wounds on every heart. Inside a charmed circle, you may steer clear, yourself, of torture and starvation and other forms of pain at its most extreme. But you still know what it's like to watch Grandma decline or cower in the bedroom while your parents quarrel or feel your gut churn when a doctor delivers bad news or an airplane flies into the World Trade Center. You know how it feels to wedge your face into the pillow's dark and weep. And you know how hard it is, when that happens, to get up in the morning and stand tall through the day.

Why should this be so? How can a plague of sighing and grief be anything but evil?

Well, it *is* evil, and it's brutal, relentless, and devastating. Deny this, or walk around too cheerful, and you are naïve and out of touch, like the famous Pollyanna. But must all of this persist? Was the world a mess from the start, and suffering built into its very fiber? Or did evil somehow sneak into an otherwise innocent domain, and is there hope that it can be overcome?

The twentieth-century American novelist Wallace Stegner made Joe Allston the central character of a book he called *All the Little Live Things.*

The Promise of Peace

The title was a reference to the natural world, and one key question the book poses is this: How does the world around you—the stuff in it, the people, the endless goings-on—affect your outlook? What does it mean for how you feel about your life, for how you dream and how you carry on?

In Stegner's story, Joe Allston and his wife have retired to California, near the San Andreas Fault, where they live off the beaten track and try to keep the bugs and gophers at bay. Allston has lived an interesting but difficult life, and he approaches his days with evident resentment. A teacher at church had once tried to convince him that the world was basically good, but Joe didn't believe it. Even at the age of eight or nine, he'd thought evil "was part of the mud life was made with," and he thought so still. The world was pitiless now, and had always been pitiless.

One day a pregnant neighbor who is also a cancer patient presses him on how he feels about "the human race." Given the circumstances humans live in and their performance so far, he is pessimistic. Allston tells his neighbor that he thinks more and more people will become hoodlums and criminals. Various underworlds of poverty and lawlessness will grow more and more dangerous. Sooner or later, someone will "push the button, or one of our improvements will backfire, and our technical tinkering will finally destroy all life, and ourselves with it."

Then Joe Allston describes the never-ending cycle that he imagines will take place. Mother Nature will start over, and the whole Darwinian drama will repeat itself. An atom will become a cell, and a cell a colony of cells. When something like the brain emerges again, new tools and languages will appear, and competition will grow more strident and once more harden into violence. Then somebody will push the button and . . . well, the whole story will repeat itself again and again.

To Joe Allston, the natural world is like Sisyphus in the Greek myth—condemned, so to speak, to an eternal punishment of pushing a stone up a hill only to see it roll down so he has to push it up again . . . and again . . . and again.

It's a thoroughly secular vision, and it's as bleak as night. Life is a treadmill. All of nature is random and indiscriminate. Anyone with confidence has a defective brain. No wonder Joe Allston tells his friend, "I do

86

not accept the universe." At one point he confesses, "I've resigned." It's as if human civilization is beneath him. It's a club he will no longer belong to; he's given up on it.[1]

What if Hope Is a Swindle?

The Bible differs from all this. In the Bible, you find passion and joy, not gloomy resignation. This book knows nothing of the Darwinian drama, and it knows nothing, either, of inevitable doom. But the Bible does know pain. Inside its pages you find characters and writers who stagger under the weight of suffering, and who struggle with how to carry on. They have moments when they wonder whether God is trustworthy and whether the promises mean anything. Sometimes they shake their fists at the heavens.

One of these is a little-known Hebrew prophet named Habakkuk. Perhaps he worked at the temple—the book that bears his name reads as though it was composed for a worship service. The Bible never tells Habakkuk's story. Still, from what he wrote, we do know that he was horrified by the destruction, contentiousness, and injustice he saw around him. And we know that while he was alive, the Babylonians, with all their cruelty and power and imperial ambition, were a threat and humiliation to the Hebrew people.

Not much is new here—not so far. The Hebrew prophets didn't run the country or have other high-profile jobs, and their life stories were often untold or little known. What's more, Hebrew prophets are famous for being horrified by bad behavior and human agony—that's nothing new. They are famous, too, for giving voice to Israel's fears about scary, nearby nations.

What's new, or at least distinctive, about Habakkuk is that he dared to express, more vividly, perhaps, than any other prophet, his doubts and his distress. The first words out of his mouth were a complaint: "O Lord, how long shall I cry for help? . . . Why do you make me . . . look at trouble?"[2] When Habakkuk heard God suggesting that marauding Babylonians might, somehow, be useful, he said in disgust, "What am I? What are we? Chopped liver?"

The American actor Jimmy Durante helped make "chopped liver"—the Jewish American side dish—a colorful reference to something insignificant, overlooked, scoffed at. Habakkuk, writing long ago, didn't know the phrase, so he said that God was treating the people of Israel like "fish of the sea" that are caught with a hook or snared with a net.

Habakkuk was bewildered. Everywhere there was evil and misery. How could God oppose these things yet consent to them? The covenant, after all, was plain. Habakkuk had read it. He knew the promises. By his lights, God should be fixing problems, yet now the *in*efficacy of prayer was the conspicuous thing. It was nothing short of flagrant.

So Habakkuk took his complaint—and the complaint of all who suffer—directly to God: "What are we? Chopped liver?"

That honesty and outspokenness belongs to the deeper spirit, actually, of the whole Bible. A softer version comes through in Psalm 73, where people chafing under the malice of the wicked wonder, " 'Is there knowledge in the Most High?' " Habakkuk's near-contemporary, Jeremiah, asks famously, "Why does the way of the guilty prosper?" As for the New Testament, it permits Jesus Himself to cry out in despair, " 'My God, my God, why have you forsaken me?' " And Paul speaks without blinking of creation's "futility," its "bondage to decay," its "groaning" right up to the present time.[3]

Dreams are deferred. Horrors happen. The Bible acknowledges all of this.

Of course, the Bible's forthrightness doesn't by itself resolve our anxieties. I'm a human being, and I want to know whether I can better my life and circumstances, and whether my children and neighbors can better theirs. How, otherwise, can anyone stand tall? How, otherwise, can we truly flourish?

As I've said from the first page of this book, every human being lives in the space between dreams and disappointments. If the evil we see in that space seems utterly unyielding—if it belongs, or seems to belong, to the mud life is made with—hope makes no sense. Against insurmountable obstacles, hope is a swindle, a self-deception, a cruel joke.

For a moment, imagine you believed this. Imagine you really believed the world was hopeless and thought your own life was a mess and couldn't get better. Then suppose that despite your pessimism you still felt the tug of moral obligation. You still felt you should do something about the imperfections in yourself and your world, still felt you should accomplish something good with your life.

With all these mixed feelings—"The world is senseless, but I must do something; nothing really matters, but I must try"—how would you cope? How would you stand tall?

Well, you might not. You might slump into melancholy. Those who do this may, in the end, bow before the savage god of suicide, or sink so far into themselves that they can't manage on their own, or merely endure the long sadness of a barely functional existence. Melancholy is tragic. You don't stand tall, you droop. Or crash.

Then again, you might cope with your mixed feelings by sheer defiance, like those gritty atheists who, despite believing that effort toward betterment is finally pointless, still hold on to the best of inherited morality. You might simply refuse, in other words, to let the harsh truth determine altogether how you feel and act. Then you'd take what satisfaction you can from small episodes—a child's response to a held-out hand; the lawn looking better for being mowed—and just do what you can to keep a stiff upper lip about the rest.

The French author Albert Camus aspired to such defiance. In his famous novel *The Plague,* he wrote about a physician named Bernard Rieux who lived in a town stricken by pestilence. The town's plight suggests the plight of all in a godless universe. Yet the conversations in the book show heartfelt allegiance to the path of sympathy, and the doctor and his acquaintances try to ease the pain and cure the sick. They wonder if you can be a "saint without God," and in the midst of this wondering, they continue to embrace the responsibility they feel to assist the unlucky people who really need them.

But the book's characters are troubled and tired. Their situation is "absurd," and they see no release from weariness—"except death." At one point, Dr. Rieux confides to a journalist that he feels a "bleak indifference steadily gaining on him."[4]

How would anyone except the very lucky—people whose childhoods and education were steadying; people gifted enough to have compelling roles—ever qualify to be one of these gritty atheists? Hope supplies energy for passion, and if you had neither hope nor truly engaging circumstances, how would you possibly find passion to live out the best of inherited morality? Camus' very honest book shows that in the face of absurdity even the well-off and well-placed must struggle against feelings of bleakness and indifference.

If in the midst of hopelessness you still felt the tug of moral obligation, you might try still another tack and begin to question the relevance of your moral feelings. In a hopeless world, why care about obligations your parents or church or school have passed on to you? How can they really matter?

One of the greatest enemies of Christian faith was the nineteenth-century philosopher Friedrich Nietzsche. He said you *can't* trust the moral judgments you inherit; it's best to deny their force. Just stop worrying about ideals someone else tells you to adopt, and get rid of the guilt. Instead, say Yes to life the way it really is. Say Yes to the struggle for mastery that is our natural bent; Yes to the "overpowering of what is alien and weaker." Acknowledge that competition is relentless and then meet it by being creative, independent, and strong. Say Yes to *self*-assertion.[5]

How do you stand tall if you think the world is hopeless? Well, on this view, you stand tall by being a winner, not a loser. Justice and mercy are fabrications—not what life is really about. To stand tall, you acknowledge that the world is not for the weak; it's for the strong. Big fish eat little fish. You simply do your best to stay on top.

The trouble is that despite efforts like this to push inherited morality out of the way, we just *do*—unless we are sociopaths—sit in judgment on ourselves and our surroundings. You may want to be rid entirely of the morality that was passed on to you, but you won't succeed. You'll just mutilate yourself trying. Who, after all, can be truly at ease with someone who pays no heed to his dying mother? Or who has as little sympathy for starving children as for dead flies? Or who takes delight in torturing homeless people?

Those who brought you up taught you to be horrified by things like this, and neither you nor anyone else can throw off everything from the past. You may make *adjustments,* like the people who said No to the slave trade or the ones who, unfortunately, said Yes to weapons of mass destruction. What you *can't* do is throw off everything you've learned or stood for. You certainly can't suddenly pretend that it's well and good to look out only for yourself and care nothing at all about the moral call placed on you by faces other than your own.[6]

So, not even the lucky and the strong can be at peace with pain in the world. Not completely. It's distasteful when people suffer. It's *especially* distasteful when God appears to look on while the suffering happens. To one degree or another, then, Habakkuk's complaint resonates with everyone.

Hope Without Explanations

What are we anyway? Chopped liver?

The Bible says No, we're not chopped liver. But as to why God puts up with so much suffering, Habakkuk, like the famously wretched Job, never gets the comfort of an explanation. Instead, he hears God declare that the time will come when all is well. God has an "end" in mind. "If it seems to tarry, wait for it; it will surely come."[7]

But waiting isn't easy. How do you cope today? If you yourself suffer; if you feel the moral call of others and want them delivered from their suffering, how do you manage now? Well, this is what God says: "Look at the proud! Their spirit is not right in them, but the righteous live by their faith."[8]

Based on the subtleties of the Hebrew language, these words—"the righteous live by their faith"—make this simple, basic point: *You can find life, and you can live justly, when you have faith in the faithfulness of God.*

The Hebrew people have always defied the temptation to sheer doom-and-gloom concerning life on earth. Often, their neighbors have not. In the surrounding world at about the time Habakkuk lived, a vision as dark as the one Joe Allston talked about was competing for attention. It is enshrined in the story the Babylonians told about how the world began, the *Enuma Elish,* as it is called. From the start, the story is unsettling.

For one thing, it takes for granted not one God but a whole multitude of gods. And what's more, these gods are cranky and quarrelsome. Ominously, they align themselves into rival forces, one led by the god Marduk and the other by Tiamat. Eventually, a climactic battle occurs. When Marduk wins, he splits the body of Tiamat in two and with one half of her creates the sky and with the other half creates the earth.

In this account, the whole world *begins in violence.*

Marduk decides to spare the lesser gods who had fought with Tiamat, but he assigns them to menial labor in the construction of the city he is building, and these lesser gods begin to fear that they are becoming slaves. So, in order to calm them down, Marduk creates what he calls a "lowly, primitive creature." Creatures of this kind will save the lesser gods from drudgery. They will be slaves so the gods "may have rest."[9]

The new creature is . . . us. The new species of slaves is . . . us.

That's how the Babylonians felt about their place in the world. The people who were threatening Judea during Habakkuk's lifetime thought human beings were slaves of the gods. They really *were* chopped liver. You can imagine that if Joe Allston had lived then, he might have said, "I don't accept the universe" and then declared his resignation from it. In a world like that, why would anyone feel good about trying to make a difference?

As for Habakkuk, he knew very well that our existence is difficult and that here on earth you sometimes feel abandoned. But Habakkuk heard God say, *You can find life, and you can live justly, when you trust in the faithfulness of God.* Not only did he hear this, but he belonged to a community that told a different story of how the world began. That made a difference, too.

The story the Hebrews recorded in the book of Genesis denies that we owe our existence to quarreling deities. We owe it instead to one God, a God who, compared with the greedy gods of Babylon, is generous and caring. This one God makes all things—and not only gives life to human beings but also offers rest and friendship.

Amazing.

The story also says that instead of everlasting toil, there will be, each week, a day of rest—a "seventh day" to share with God, with a God who wants and enjoys our company. And we are by no means slaves on the other days of the week, but we are God's junior partners, created in the divine "image" so we can be creative too. Because of this, we can "till" and "keep" the garden that is in the making. Because of it, we can give "names" to the animals—and otherwise set about creating human culture.[10]

This is the story the Hebrews told. To them, it was the background for all the promises of God: our world *made by Someone who is generous;* our world *hospitable to human dreams and human strivings.*

The Hebrews, in other words, felt no contempt for human flesh and human circumstances. Far from it. The world, after all, was God's, and the creation a gift and blessing. Even amid suffering—even when their hearts were melting like wax and their bodies were so thin they could count the bones—they spoke "praise in the great congregation," believed that "dominion belongs to the LORD," embraced the prospect of "deliverance."

These last words come from Psalm 22, the very psalm Jesus was quoting at His execution when He cried out, "My God, my God, why have you forsaken me?"[11] The sentiment they express is like that of Paul, who saw "futility" and "groaning" all around him, yet held on to hope. The "sufferings of this present time," he believed, were like "labor pains," and "not worth comparing" to what is yet in store for us.[12]

The sentiment is also like that you find in the book of Revelation. Amid his own and his church's suffering, the author proclaimed "a new heaven and a new earth," where "crying and pain will be no more." And earlier, in a scene of heavenly praise, he declared the basis for his confidence. Here worshipers sing "without ceasing" to a "holy" God who is "worthy" of "glory and honor and power." For You "created all things," these worshipers exclaim, "and by your will they existed and were created."[13]

With their Creation story, the Hebrew people made the world a theater of divine glory and human opportunity. It was, in its beginning and in its essence, a world of peace and beauty. The possibilities were spell-binding, and nothing in earth or heaven could finally defeat those possibilities: God was in charge.

But in making junior partners, God made men and women free. They weren't puppets; they could chart a course. And Genesis goes on to tell how self-regard came in, how hearts turned away from the Creator, how the desire to flourish became a blight of rivalry, how the human family broke apart through envy and murderous revenge.

All this was "sin"—a revolt against God that would come to feel like an evil power "lurking at the door," like something that can take possession of you. And it was so disastrous that it could cast its dark spell even on the earth itself. In the Genesis story, Adam hears God say, " 'Cursed is the ground because of you.' "[14]

Still, hope remains. Evil has sneaked in, but the transfiguration of all things is sure. Because God is our Maker, "the creation itself," as Paul said, "will be set free from its bondage to decay," and God's life-giving presence will conquer suffering and at last bring about even "the redemption of our bodies."[15]

You are Pollyanna if you think it's easy to believe all this, easy to be so trustful. Too many bad things happen too often. I heard a young woman, a graduate of an Adventist college, tell a group of older Christians, "Searching for faith is not a walk in the park for us." Neither is keeping the faith you find.

Even the great spiritual leaders of Israel understood this. The prophet Habakkuk knew it as well as anyone—knew what Ellen White echoed centuries later when she said that "finite beings" can never fully comprehend the "mysteries" of God.[16] Despite this, Habakkuk listened when God responded to his—and every thoughtful person's—complaint. He listened, and what he heard were words of hope. A voice declared, *You can find life, and you can live justly, when you trust in the faithfulness of God.*

This had to ring a bell—it's what the Hebrew Creation story, with its likening of human beings to their kind and generous Maker, seemed to say. And according to the story Habakkuk tells, he now heard more of what this means. Through all of chapter 2—the middle of his book—God's moral passion and high expectations pierce the darkness. You, God says in effect, need not live on "evil gain." You need not build your world "by bloodshed." You are called to be "just," and you can be just.

Habakkuk still doesn't understand. But once more, despite his questions and despite his bewilderment, he says Yes to God. He says Yes to the Voice that declares, *You can find life, and you can live justly, when you trust in the faithfulness of God.* He affirms once more that God *will* come forth to "save."[17]

Gloomy visions make for barbarity. The Babylonians were gloomy, and in their gloom, they thought only of asserting themselves. Today the Darwinian darkness—the presumption that nature, "red in tooth and claw," turns the Creator's love into make-believe—looms large in human consciousness.[18] And with its specter of pitiless struggle and final futility, it, too, is gloomy. Save for the spiritual resources built up over centuries of confidence in the biblical vision, that darkness would today overwhelm generosity and make the just life a refuge for losers. Where gloom has prevailed as it did in Babylon and later in Greece and Rome, the ethic of conquest has been largely unchecked, and the fate of the vulnerable largely unaddressed.

So when the heroes of Scripture embrace a different story of beginnings, they embrace a different way of being. In the temple, Habakkuk heard the long-told narratives of deliverance from exile, and in the temple, he learned and sang the poetry of praise. Even as he dealt with suffering, he heard the testimony of the trusting. Even as he failed to understand the ways of God, he felt the plausibility of God's love.

Today, the community of faith embraces the Habakkuk tradition with reasons as good as his were. These reasons don't deliver us from doubt; but despite the questions and bewilderment, we can still say Yes—Yes to God, and Yes to the just life that God inspires.

All this is a kind of defiance, a refusal to sink into the dark suspicion of the jungle. It is why Habakkuk, the man who was honest to God, renews the human heart. It is why his last words ring out like bells on Easter morning:

Though the fig tree does not blossom,
    and no fruit is on the vines;
though the produce of the olive fails,
    and the fields yield no food;
though the flock is cut off from the fold
    and there is no herd in the stalls,
yet I will rejoice in the LORD;
    I will exult in the God of my salvation.
God, the Lord, is my strength;
    he makes my feet like the feet of a deer,
and makes me tread upon the heights.[19]

The man who was honest to God is strong and joyful in the end. And the point is that you and I can be strong and joyful too.

1. Wallace Stegner, *All the Little Live Things* (New York: Viking Press, 1967). The first quote is from the beginning of chapter II; the conversation with the pregnant neighbor is from section 5 of chapter IV.

2. Habakkuk 1:2, 3.

3. The quotes are from Psalm 73:10–12, from Jeremiah 12:1, from Matthew 27:46 (also Mark 15:34), and from Romans 8:20–22.

4. Albert Camus, *The Plague*, First Vintage International Edition, trans. Stuart Gilbert (New York: Vintage Books, 1991), 253–255. The last quote is from ibid., 91.

5. The quoted words are from Friedrich Nietzsche, *Beyond Good and Evil*, trans. Walter Kaufmann (New York: Vintage Books, 1966), 203.

6. For this and the previous paragraph, I learned much from William Greenway, "Charles Taylor on Affirmation, Mutilation, and Theism: A Retrospective Reading of *Sources of the Self*," *Journal of Religion* 80 (January 2000): 23–40.

7. Habakkuk 2:3.

8. Habakkuk 2:4. For the interpretation of this verse, I rely on Francis I. Andersen, *Habakkuk*, Anchor Bible (New Haven: Yale University Press, 2001), 199ff.

9. I rely for my telling of the Babylonian creation epic on D. Winton Thomas, ed. and trans., *Documents from the Old Testament Times* (New York: Harper & Row, 1958), 3–16.

10. The quotes, in the order of their appearance, are from Genesis 2:3; 1:26; 2:15; 2:20.

11. Quotes are from Psalm 22:25, 28, 31. Jesus' words are from verse 1.

12. These phrases are from Romans 8:18–25.

13. From Revelation 21:1, 4; 4:8–11.

14. The image of sin "lurking at the door" is from God's words to Cain in Genesis 4:7. The second quote is from Genesis 3:17.

15. See Romans 8:21–23.

16. Ellen White, *Steps to Christ* (Washington, D.C.: Review and Herald®, 1892), 106.

17. Habakkuk 2:9, 12; then 2:4; finally, 3:13.

18. The famous phrase is from canto LVI of Alfred, Lord Tennyson's poem *In Memoriam A. H. H.*

19. Habakkuk 3:17–19.

8

Jesus Saves

I'm preoccupied with myself. I lack sympathy for others. Questions about the "common good" bore and bother me; talk of human need exhausts my patience. I resent—or hate, or even want to hurt—some people.

God loves me anyway.

Others take me for granted. The rich exploit my labor and funnel money to themselves. Criminals want to break into my house or steal my identity or corrupt my children. So-called leaders, with egos like trucks, stand ready to nuke my city or send suicide bombers to my shopping mall.

God loves them too. Anyway.

The sense of falling short hangs over everyone. We fall short ourselves, and we see others fall short. As a result, we suffer and see others suffer, sometimes a lot. Still, God persists in loving us—loving us *and* them. This is the good news of God, or what Christians call the gospel.

God's love for us is pure reassurance and renews our hearts and hopes. God's love of others is pure challenge and calls us to love people, even unpleasant or alarming people, instead of ignoring them or pushing them away. Both points reflect God's amazing generosity, or grace. And both became unforgettably concrete—tangible enough, that is, to leave a lasting mark and make a lasting difference—through the ministry of Jesus the Nazarene.

Or so Christians say.

In one way, of course, Jesus was a failure. He made a difference in individual lives. As the authorities showed by their skittish and resentful attentions, He even made a difference for the religious and political culture of His day. Still, when the resentments of those authorities resulted in Jesus' execution, He died alone, mostly abandoned by the followers He had tried to energize.

But just when it seemed that He would leave no legacy, He was visible again—through His suddenly revitalized followers. Now they were announcing that Jesus had broken through the grave and appeared to them and commissioned them to keep His vision alive. Now, overcome by the Resurrection, they felt *saved*—saved from death and fear and hate; saved from self-obsession and self-pity; saved from lackluster lives. In a word, they felt saved from *sin*. And now, enlivened for discipleship, they wanted to make a difference the way Jesus had made a difference. Now they wanted to go to the ends of the earth telling their story, enlarging the circle of compassion, making peace.

The first believers were a new community bound together by this breathtaking reversal of fortune. But though they were euphoric and bold at times, they could still be unhappy and afraid too. They were still as human as we are and felt the needs and yearnings our own hearts know. They still lived in the space between dreams and disappointments, the space where promises matter and you want more than anything a reason to stand tall and move forward.

But it seemed to them that the Great Promise—the promise of universal blessing—was now, in some new sense, assured. Through passionate service and painful setbacks, Jesus had become, they now felt, *the* One to guide their feet " 'into the way of peace' "[1]—*the* One, that is, to bring the best and deepest human hopes to their fulfillment.

That made all the difference. In a way more profound and more satisfying than ever before, they would now live their lives in the light of the Great Promise that had animated Abraham and Moses and the prophets and Jesus Himself. The promise of peace, as interpreted by Jesus, had liberated them for a new and surprising adventure. They were like kept hawks freed to soar, but *they* would neither hurt nor destroy. Imperfect and vulnerable, they were at the same time forgiven and newly assured of God's care. And now they were going to embody that same forgiveness and that same care. They would be, by God's grace, "ambassadors for Christ"—the representatives on earth of the One who had saved their lives.[2]

Jesus, the Radical Jew

How could this happen? What made people think of Jesus as Savior of the world? What made them worship Him as the human face of . . . God?

When Jesus' public ministry began, everyone took it for granted, as Paul would later say, that He was "born of a woman." He had the same abilities and appetites—and the same temptations—as other human beings.[3] But compared with others, He had a compelling vision. And what is more, He was generous beyond all ordinary expectation—generous to a fault, as His critics would come to think.

Another thing everyone took for granted was His family history. Jesus was born a Jew, and He grew up in an observant Jewish family. You know from chapter 3 that the history of the Jews goes back to Abraham, who got past complaints about the human condition, which were then the norm, to something more hopeful—namely, the embrace of *possibility*. Out of the trust God gave him, Abraham believed he could make a difference. By living well, he and his children would become a *blessing* to all the families of the earth.[4]

Those who came after Abraham—the liberator Moses, the great prophets, and other leaders—trusted God's promise of a new day. They all knew the pain in human life, but they fixed their attention on the promise and became, against whatever obstacle, prophets of renewal, agents of change. They were God's *partners*—bound together by God's pledge to them, and by theirs to God and one another. Inside this "covenant," as it was called, they were ready to make a difference by being different. They would be originals, not just copies of the wider culture.

They would be *in*, but not exactly *of*, the world around them.

Jesus grew up inside this covenant. So it was natural that He should be familiar with the stories, festivals, and hopes of the Jewish people. His public ministry began when He was about thirty, not long after baptism sharpened His will to live as God's "beloved Son."[5] Given this commitment, it isn't surprising that, early on, He came to His hometown and addressed a Jewish synagogue on Sabbath. Nor is it surprising that He read that day from Isaiah 58 and 61, where the prophet said God's will was good news to poor people and to those who were captive or blind or oppressed.[6] These ideas belonged to the prophetic vision. They were at the heart of the Jewish heritage.

Luke's story of that Sabbath in the synagogue shows that Jesus marched to a drumbeat that was at once attractive and—to conventional minds—off-putting. He was like the prophets who before Him suffered abuse as well as praise for what they said. That day, those in attendance at first "spoke well of him." But then he said that Elijah and Elisha, both prophets of old, had reached out to a Gentile widow and a Gentile leper. The implication that the good news was for non-Jews as well as Jews enraged His listeners, and they seized Him and came close, but for the grace of God, to hurling Him off a cliff.

Jesus was a radical Jew. To outsiders in His society, what He said and did was as welcome as daylight. But to insiders, who had privileges most people didn't, His words and deeds were unsettling, His generosity offensive. The current state of things, He said, was on its way out. Even the most powerful would lose their unfair advantage. Even the people whom the insiders hated or looked down upon would be forgiven and embraced. Even the poor and powerless, women and men alike, would have a voice. And now the benchmark for true humanity, foreshadowed by the great prophets, would be this: You are truly blessed when you serve or even suffer on behalf of others. You please God when your love reaches out not only to your friends but also to your enemies.[7]

Insiders found all this increasingly hard to take. But Jesus never veered from His conviction that a saving handful—He once called His followers a "little flock"[8]—could have wide impact for the good. A saving handful living out the highest ideals could break the habit of indifference and undermine the rule of violence. A saving handful could break the in-group/out-group mentality and turn the world toward peace.

Again, it was a thought rooted in the heritage of Abraham: the hope that a mere family, or, as prophets would later say, a mere "remnant," could bear a world-changing torch. By prayer and peacemaking, all this could happen.

Life at the heart of the mission would be wonderful—a blessing and a joy, a defeat for fear and boredom. However, and Jesus Himself made the point, it would never be easy. In His manner and passion and confidence, He embodied the "abundant" life.[9] At the same time, He knew sorrow—disappointment over friends who misunderstood Him and enemies who hated His mission and wanted to destroy Him. In the short span of His public ministry, Jesus carried His message from Galilee in the north to His culture's capital, Jerusalem. He attracted followers, and crowds came to pin their hope on Him. But in Jerusalem, the authorities, aided by Judas, who belonged to the inner circle of twelve disciples, finally arrested Him. In the end, Jesus was executed in the Roman fashion, on a cross.

The Cross, Then the Resurrection

How could someone who died such a death make a lasting difference? How could such a person *save* the world?

Luke tells us that when Jesus looked down at His executioners, He prayed, " 'Father, forgive them; for they do not know what they are doing.' " Paul, while he was still railing against the new sect of Christian believers, heard Stephen, the first Christian martyr, echo these words in a prayer for those who were casting stones at him.[10] Later, Paul, now a believer himself, would write in his letter to the Romans that "God proves his love for us in that while we still were sinners"—still "enemies" of God—"Christ died for us."[11]

The first evangelists for the Christian faith saw death—or death of a certain kind—as an expression of forgiveness and acceptance. According to John, as elsewhere in the Gospels, the twelve disciples repeatedly fell short. They misunderstood and even resisted Jesus' mission. Yet when Jesus sensed that His execution was close at hand, He let the disciples know that He was laying down His life for His "friends." Despite their imperfect records, they could still be His confidantes and collaborators, still bear fruit, "fruit that will last," in His cause.[12] As Jesus' prayer on the cross suggests, even those who carried out the execution had the potential, nevertheless, to become His allies in peacemaking.

For anyone, all this can be an inspiration. Here was a Man who would pay the ultimate price in order to heal human hurt and help people flourish. He would give Himself to the cause of life and love. He would seek reconciliation instead of discord. He would stand tall for the covenant of peace. And what is more, He would stick to the mission—His heaven-sent call—no matter what. Not indifference, not rejection, not even violence would deter Him. He would prefer perilous solidarity with God to an easier way. And within that solidarity, He would, as John reports that He said, "draw all people" to Himself, to His cause, His passion, His abundant life.[13]

The sheer beauty of such a story is compelling. Here is Someone who would no more give up on you than the father who, in Jesus' famous parable, *ran out* to welcome a son who had shamed the family and squandered its resources. The son's homecoming was, as is usually said, the "return of the prodigal," but the story's center is the aging parent and his infinite regard for a child who had by no means earned the glad reception that he got.[14] Jesus' own life, it turned out, was a parable of the same love, the same inexhaustible compassion. His way of being spoke as unforgettably as did His stories. He simply loved people—*anyway.*

Yet Jesus died young—young and practically alone. This good and beautiful life came, or so it seemed, to nothing. Again, how can Jesus save us? How can His life and death—both of them, according to Paul—somehow heal the wounds we suffer from?

Well, Jesus cannot heal our wounds—cannot, that is, unless the Resurrection actually happened and actually defeated His death. By no stretch can the Cross alone be a *saving* event. By itself, an execution this ghastly and senseless shows little more than the horrific ruthlessness of depraved power. Alone, it's just evidence that, against the great machine of death and hate, life and love can make no headway and have no future. Paul himself declared, "If Christ has not been *raised,* your faith is futile and you are still in your sins."[15]

It is, of course, a matter of *faith.* No one can know with utter certainty that Jesus came forth from the grave. The idea goes against ordinary expectation. And just because of that, doubt entered in from the very start. Luke says that on the day after the Sabbath, women who had followed Jesus found the stone rolled away from the tomb and heard two angels say that He was alive. But when they told their story to the disciples and "all the rest," those who heard them said it was "an idle tale" and "did not believe them." According to John, the disciple Thomas didn't at first believe the other disciples who said that Jesus had appeared to them. Matthew reports that one day the "eleven" (the inner circle had lost Judas to suicide) met the resurrected Jesus in Galilee. There they heard Him commission them to worldwide witness on His behalf. Even at this high moment, however, "some doubted."[16]

But faith, remember, is first of all trust. Ellen White remarks that the "evidence" to base it on is "sufficient," but not so compelling as to remove "the possibility of doubt."[17] You can *trust,* in other words, but you can't *know,* not the way you know the uses of a shovel or the color of your shirt. And even among the disciples themselves, some had a harder time with trust than others did. Some doubted. But Matthew gives no suggestion—none at all—that Jesus cast the doubters aside or even scolded them. The commission to bear witness and to make disciples "of all nations" went out even to those who brought their questions with them.

Within the Jesus circle, then, the welcome extends to those who doubt as well as those who struggle in other ways. The only requirement—and now we come to the other side of faith—is commitment to the mission. Faith is trust. Faith is also commitment. As for the evidence to base it on, the Resurrection was, and is, the bedrock. Proofs of that event elude everyone today, but those who first said it was real bore a striking testimony, and their lives and legacy gave the ring of truth to what they said.

So, nothing matters more than the Resurrection. No one in the New Testament breathes a sigh of relief at Jesus' death. No one declares that if He "has not been *executed,* you are still in your sins." The cross was not even a visual symbol in church art until some four hundred years after Jesus, and when it appeared the first time, it was in a remote place—on a Roman church's wooden door.[18] This seems surprising now, but the reason, in large part, is that the cross, by itself, is not the linchpin. The whole drama of Jesus' life is what matters, and the whole drama matters because of the startling affirmation that Jesus arose from the dead. Hope is the point. The Resurrection is the linchpin.

So what does this mean for how Jesus saves?

As the inkling of resurrection grew into settled conviction, the first believers began to realize that *God* was in the Jesus story. This was far more than a titillating notion. It was a life-changing answer to a life-changing question. Who *is* at the bottom of things? What *is* the identity of God?

You might think God is like a prison warden watching for your every misstep or a retiree who has stopped working and left for the seaside or a Pharaoh who values your back and crushes your heart. From the beginning, however, Abraham and his descendants had held a different idea—namely, that God actually cares about humanity and takes steps to help and wants everyone to flourish. With the Resurrection, the first believers came to believe that this God was *personified* in Jesus.

Jesus' life had been astonishing—a life for others, full of compassion and empty of violence, acquainted with grief yet abounding with hope. The Resurrection was the divine validation of *this* life. As Paul said to the Christians in Rome, Jesus had descended from David "according to the flesh," yet He was "declared to be the Son of God . . . by resurrection from the dead."[19]

Jesus had given much. When His gifts were spurned, He had given again. And now the Resurrection made His astonishing life all the more astonishing. Now the first followers began to feel that you could see in Jesus the beauty of divine love. Here the story of God and the story of humanity seemed somehow to converge. In this one life—the one life

God declared without qualification to be His own—the divine and human stories, as one theologian said, were "at last indivisibly one."[20]

So the Letter to the Colossians can say concerning Jesus, "He is the image of the invisible God." And in words most startling, the Gospel of John can say that He was God made "flesh," the revelation of the Father's heart. This was at a time when the Roman emperor wanted people to think that *he* was "god-manifest."[21] What the New Testament writers said about Jesus was thus a rebuke of the dominant politics, and it took courage to say it. Still, God's true colors, said the first Christians, are what you see in Jesus, not what you see in Caesar.

No one forgot, though, that Jesus was born of a woman and descended from the very human David. Jesus was "like his brothers and sisters in every respect." When He was a child, He asked questions and "increased" in understanding. He was "tested" by what He suffered. He "learned obedience."[22]

So here was Someone like you and me—who, by the Father's grace was so fully responsive to divine leading that He was the *human form of who God is.* In Him you could see the *identity* of God. In Him you could see, too, the *identity* of the truly human; He was the One whose loyalty to God and service to others set the standard for everyone, the One who led Paul to say, "Let the same mind be in you that was in Christ Jesus."[23]

The Devil's Downfall

Many things are beyond explaining. The Resurrection, and all it means, is one of them. Still, a community of faith sprang up, convinced not only that Jesus was alive but also that through Him everything was changing for the better. As the New Testament says, people once alienated from the Maker of all things were coming to feel at home—"reconciled" to God through Christ. People once caught in the death trap of failure and fear were newly "alive" through the gift of God's grace. People once divided into hostile camps were finding "peace." Now, unjust "rulers and authorities" appeared vulnerable: Christ had put their greed and surliness to shame. Now, a death that had seemed senseless and discouraging felt like the death knell for death; it had struck a decisive blow to the devil, who has "the power of death," and to all the devil's "works."[24]

The whole purpose of what happened in Jesus had come clear: through *this* life, *this* sacrifice for others, *this* resurrection, God, as Paul writes, had demonstrated the divine "righteousness." God had shown, in other words, the compassion and faithfulness that, no matter what, stay true to human need, true to the Great Promise made to Abraham on behalf of all humanity. The "power of sin," Paul had said, puts goodness and blessing at risk. It leaves people dishonest, unkind, out of touch with " 'the way of peace.' " But God looks past sin to possibility. Through the grace embodied in the whole story of Jesus, everyone can acknowledge mistakes and shortfalls, confident that God forgives.[25] And from a place of forgiveness and acceptance, everyone can embrace the new life of faith and find strength to love as Jesus did. Everyone can resist the wider world and "pursue what makes for peace," what truly blesses others, what truly helps humanity find fulfillment for its best and deepest wishes.[26]

The Jesus story said, in dramatic fashion, that God's amazing generosity is the first, or basic, truth. Grace is at the bottom of things. This means acceptance by God, whose love cannot be quashed even by our own resistance to it. And it also means opportunity—opportunity to walk the same path and find the same joy as Jesus did.

You can refuse this opportunity. After all, it is dangerous. Jesus said true disciples would "take up their cross" like He did. But the opportunity is also wonderfully satisfying. Instead of being, as some think, a dismal obsession with sin, Christian life is a ministry of reconciliation and a passion for peace. You and your partners in faith become "ambassadors" for Christ. You speak the good news of grace. After the *shalom* ideal, you do what you can to bring food, freedom, and safety to *all* God's children. You break down dividing walls. You help people caught between their dreams and disappointments to flourish nevertheless and to be fully alive.[27]

Jesus doesn't squelch desire. He redirects it—away from restless jealousy of neighbor into an impassioned defense of life for everyone. In Christ, God "sanctifies" you—sets you apart, takes possession of your heart.[28] And all this is so you will fulfill the divine purpose, so you will be light against the uncomprehending dark, so you will become God's partner in the covenant of peace and help to bring prosperity and well-being to all.

New desire and new passion arising from new hope—these are the gifts God bestows through Christ. The divine energy that brought Jesus back from the grave renews human life today. Paul, a once violent man who was now a missionary and a peacemaker, said that "by the grace of God I am what I am." He was, to be sure, no puppet. Grace didn't mean that God was pulling the strings and Paul's actions were not his own. He was fully responsible for what he did. But his transformed life, lived out "in the flesh," was still, he wrote, God's gift. New life was a reason, every day, to be amazed and grateful.[29]

The Resurrection was a defeat for lackluster existence and a victory for the vision that Abraham had pioneered. He had said No to the complaint, then commonplace, that fate is given and cannot be changed. He had said Yes to the promise that lives of blessing can transform possibilities for everyone.

The Resurrection was a defeat, too, for the power of death and for the devil, who has that power. Jesus was raised from the dead, and that is a guarantee that the door to resurrection is open to others. Death is the "last enemy," Paul said, but *it will be destroyed.* As he told the Corinthians, "the dead will be raised imperishable, and we will be changed."[30]

This, too, was a reason for amazement and gratitude. And like the rest of the Good News in the Jesus story, it was a tremendous motivator. The Resurrection put the Crucifixion in a new light, and from the new vantage point it was clear that killing Jesus had been futile—like trying to destroy the seed head of a dandelion by blowing on it. Not only was Christ now "exalted at the right hand of God,"[31] He was also continuing to exist in this world. He was here *as* the new (and spreading) community of Christians. These early Christians understood, after all, that you are not meant to sit and marvel at the Jesus story. You are meant to *be* the next chapter, to *be* nothing less than the ongoing ministry of Christ on earth.

Jesus not only saves but continues to save.

And that brings us to what I call the "beloved community," the next theme of Christian life and teaching we are going to consider.

---

1. Luke 1:79.

2. See 2 Corinthians 5:16–21.

3. See Galatians 4:4 and Hebrews 4:15.

4. See Genesis 12:1–4.

5. Luke 3:21, 22. I here use the phrase familiar from the King James Version.

6. Luke 4:16–30.

7. See Matthew 5, and then consider, besides the call of Abraham (in Genesis 12:1–4), the vision expressed in Isaiah 2:2–4 (no more war), or in Isaiah 19:23–25 (God will bless Egypt and Assyria), or in Jeremiah 29:1–7 (seek the welfare of the Babylonian city where you live), or in Isaiah 52:13–53:12 (redemptive nonviolence; suffering that heals), or in Jonah 3:10 and 4:11 (care for even the hated Assyrians in Nineveh).

8. Luke 12:32.

9. In John 10:10, Jesus famously remarks, " 'I came that they may have life, and have it abundantly.' "

10. Luke 23:34; cf. Acts 7:60.

11. Romans 5:8, 10.

12. For the disciples' imperfection in John, see John 6:70, 71; 12:4, 5; 14:9; 16:32. Yet Jesus still considers them His "friends."

13. John 12:32.

14. See Luke 15:11–32.

15. See Romans 5:6–10 for Paul's perspective on the life and death of Jesus. First Corinthians 15:17 is the striking sentence about the Resurrection; emphasis added.

16. Luke 24:1–12, 23; John 20:24–29; Matthew 27:3–5; 28:16–20.

17. Ellen G. White, *Steps to Christ* (Washington, D.C.: Review and Herald®, 1892), 105.

18. In *Civilization: A Personal View* (New York: Harper & Row, 1969), 29, historian Kenneth Clark locates the "first example" of the cross in a Christian church. It is "in a corner, almost out of sight" on the doors of Santa Sabina, a church in Rome. It dates to about 430 C.E.

19. Romans 1:3, 4.

20. In Zechariah 9, a key passage for the first Christians, the prophet's vision of the coming Peacemaker ends with this exclamation (verse 17) of praise to God: "For what goodness and beauty are his!" The quoted phrase is from James Wm. McClendon Jr., *Doctrines: Systematic Theology*, vol. 2 (Nashville: Abingdon, 1994), 276, where it is italicized.

21. Colossians 1:15; John 1:14, 18. On the imperial cult's view of Caesar, see Brian J. Walsh and Sylvia C. Keesmaat, *Colossians Remixed: Subverting the Empire* (Downers Grove, Ill.: InterVarsity Press, 2004), 90.

22. Hebrews 2:17, 18; 5:8; Luke 2:46, 52.

23. Philippians 2:5.

24. On being "reconciled" with God through Christ, 2 Corinthians 5:18, 19; on resurrection, grace, and peace, Ephesians 2:1–10, 14, 15; on Christ's disarming, and "triumphing over," the rulers, Colossians 2:15; on His victory over death and the works of the devil, Hebrews 2:14, 15; 1 John 3:8.

25. Romans 3:9–18, 21–25. Paul writes as a Jew, and the parallelism of the Hebrew poetry in, e.g., Psalm 143:1, 11, 12, shows that for a Jew, "righteousness" would be roughly similar to "faithfulness," or "steadfast love." Paul alludes to the Great Promise of Genesis 12:3 in Romans 4:13 and also in Galatians 3:8.

26. I allude to Romans 12 and quote Romans 14:19.

27. On discipleship and the Cross, see Mark 8:34 and 10:37–39; on the "ministry of reconciliation" as "ambassadors for Christ," see 2 Corinthians 5:20; for the *shalom* ideal, see Ezekiel 34:25–31.

28. See John 17:17–19; and compare Romans 6, where God liberates us from sin and that new state is called "sanctification" (verse 22).

29. For Paul's words, see 1 Corinthians 15:10 and Galatians 2:20.

30. See 1 Corinthians 15 for a long meditation on the Resurrection. The quoted phrases are from 15:26, 52.

31. So Peter declared on the Day of Pentecost, according to Acts 2:33. The dandelion seed head comparison I saw first somewhere in the writings of Walter Wink.

9

The Beloved Community

The church is the beloved community, and the beloved community is
. . . a mess. But it is also the body of the risen and returning Christ. It is
Christ existing on earth today. And thanks to this body—this community, these people—Jesus not only saves but continues to save.

That's what Christians say, but how can this be?

Consider the congregation Paul founded in Corinth. The city itself
was a commercial crossroads, a seaport with a seaport's doubtful morals.
Pagan temples were commonplace; statues of pagan gods studded the
streets. Yet here some Jews and more Gentiles became the city's fledgling
Christian community. After eighteen months, Paul left Corinth to continue his missionary travels. When he wrote his first letter back to Corinth
a few years later, the community of Christians he'd come to love was rife
with lawsuits, sexual sin, and quarrels over doctrine, idols, and food.

So this congregation, dating back to the beginnings of Christianity,
was itself . . . a mess. Still, Paul could assure the members that God had
chosen *them* to shame and overturn the evil powers.[1] God had chosen
them to change the world.

Again, how can this be?

It's easy enough to see why problems come into Christian churches.
The faith experience itself is difficult. When you pledge commitment to
Christ, you say you will keep the commandments of God and the faith

of Jesus. But with a standard this high, you fall short—even the best-intentioned and most self-disciplined fall short. And because you feel it's *God* you're letting down, you fret about this, perhaps a lot. If you're someone who attends more to God's commands than to God's assurance of forgiveness, you may turn into a worrywart and suffer from salvation anxiety. In this condition, you're obsessed with how you're doing and afraid of what God thinks.

How do you cope? You may withdraw into yourself. Or boost your own self-estimate by finding fault with others. Or give up on your high ideals and lapse into a less caring life. And with any of these, you give misery—your own and that of others—a new toehold. If enough members of a congregation are similarly anxious and cope in similar ways, you end up with a mess—a congregation torn apart by injury and discord.

What happens inside the faith experience is one thing. Pressures from outside make trouble too. The beloved community exists, always, within a surrounding, and often hostile, culture. In Corinth at the time the church was getting started, pagan religion spoke of gods replete with wants, lacking in compassion, and indifferent to human need. That left human supplicants scrambling for favor and focused on themselves, and it made them more manipulative than caring in their daily interactions. People of more secular bent, less preoccupied with the gods, tried to find better lives through "wisdom," or self-examination. The Stoic writer Seneca, for example, could speak of the "delightful" sleep that comes when, at day's end, you reflect critically on how you have done. "I avail myself of this privilege," he said, "and every day I plead my cause before the bar of self."[2]

But for Paul, the alternatives to Christ crucified and raised were dead ends. Pagan self-obsession was unacceptable. As for Stoic "wisdom," it neither offered hope nor commended love—certainly not the love that reaches out to others, including those most vulnerable. In the surrounding culture, the bar was set too low, and the God of Jesus Christ was a stark alternative. The wider world didn't see kindness at the heart of things and didn't hear the call to human kindness that Christians heard.

Still, even though the gospel had come to the church in Corinth, trouble remained. True faith was difficult. What is more, the pressure from outside was still felt inside, taking the edge off of loyalty to Christ, diminishing people into less than what they could be.

All this—the worrying, the stale sanctimony, the lowered standards— all this comes into the church, then and now, like poison. But there is a cure for it, and the cure is heartfelt embrace of what we considered before, the Good News that Jesus saves. Once the beloved community grasps this Good News fully—and not least its message of forgiveness— it becomes, despite all its faults, one of the great marvels of divine grace.

This was so even in the church at Corinth. The discord was palpable, the flaws as plain as mud, but newness of life was evident too. Some of them, Paul said, were "idolaters," some promiscuous, some "drunkards" and "revilers" and "robbers." "But you were washed, you were sanctified, you were justified in the name of the Lord Jesus Christ and in the Spirit of our God."[3] Members had received God's gifts—been forgiven, changed, set apart for service. Now they had a vision for their lives that was, in both scope and depth, amazing.

So, inside the church at Corinth, God was making bad people into better people. For all its problems, this fledgling Christian community was still a place where hope ran deep and imagination was like a beacon cutting through the dark, helping people see what they would otherwise fail to see. You found problems in the church—on earth they never go away and never cease to hurt. But you found the story of Jesus, too, and you found a people emboldened by that story to rethink what they had done and thought, and to begin to live their best and deepest dreams.

Paul's confidence about all this was sufficient, as we saw, for him to say that the church is a community God-chosen for the purpose of overturning evil. When in the company of others you are part of the church, you are, as Paul's second letter would say, Christ's "ambassadors"— agents of the very "reconciliation" that is God's own mission in the world.[4]

This had been the idea from day one. The risen Jesus, Luke tells us, assured His disciples that they would become His "witnesses," both at home and "to the ends of the earth."[5] By God's grace, it wasn't long until these witnesses established, in Jerusalem, a community of people who, with "glad and generous hearts,"[6] were attempting to *be* Christ on earth. They were praising God together, taking care of one another, pursuing a ministry of healing deeds and words.

And all the while, they were growing—finding new members, taking the story to the wider world, enlarging the circle of compassion. Later, Paul would say the baptism that converts underwent was a baptism "into Christ Jesus." By this rite they became one with Christ—their old selves were "buried" and new selves were "raised from the dead" so that, in the company of one another, they could "walk in newness of life."[7]

As Jesus, at His own baptism, had come to see Himself as God's "beloved son," so these new Christians came to see themselves as God's beloved children.[8] And as Jesus, fortified by this love and aflame with new purpose, had sought to renew vision and heal humanity, so did these new Christians. They came to see, indeed, that in responding to the grace and peace of Christ, they would change the world. They would change it by keeping the commandments of God and the faith of Jesus.

All this they would *dare* to do. They had embraced the Good News that Jesus saves, and now, despite problems, they would put it into practice. God's grace had galvanized their whole community to aspiration and adventure.

Practicing Community

Suzie is the nurse in *Wit,* the Pulitzer Prize–winning play about a fifty-year-old English professor who is dying from ovarian cancer. One day Suzie brings a Popsicle into the hospital room, and her patient gladly accepts half of it. Then, taking a seat on the commode by her patient's bedside, the nurse tells this story: "When I was a kid, we used to get these from a truck. The man would come around and ring his bell and we'd all run over. Then we'd sit on the curb and eat our Popsicles."

She pauses.

"Pretty profound, huh?"[9]

Suzie's story *is* profound. It's profound because when you do something together with others and do it repeatedly, the experience sticks with you and affects your whole outlook. It shapes how you see the world, how you feel about it, how you carry out your daily life. That's why, from the beginning, the beloved community put *shared practices* at the center of their lives. Doing things together and doing them repeatedly was a key strategy for keeping focused on God and on God's will and way.

So the first thing to say about practicing the Good News is that it's about doing certain things *together*. Much of popular Christianity thinks of a "relationship with Christ" as a personal—almost a private—matter. The relationship is not so much a God-connection you and others share as one you have on your own. For people who think this way, it is more natural to speak and sing of *my* Savior than to speak and sing of *ours*; the words *I* and *me* roll off the tongue more easily than *we* and *us*.

This bent reflects the individualism of today's Western culture and its obsession with independence and personal choice. The most mature human beings, it is thought, are the ones who thrust off dependence on others. Autonomy is the ideal. For Christians who accept all this uncritically, a relationship with God may seem to depend little, or not at all, on a relationship with other human beings.

But the first accounts of the church show men and women linked inseparably with one another. Autumn leaves piled together withstand the wind; solitary leaves do not. The first Christians understood this—understood, as Richard Rice declares, that "belonging" is the key. Wherever they went, they established *communities*. Solo religiosity—I-do-it-my-way "spirituality"—would have been, to them, as foreign as fast food.[10] Through constant connection and through activities that reinforced it, they withstood the pressures that might otherwise have scattered them into insignificance. Together, they kept their memories alive; they resisted the dominant culture; they strengthened their resolve against indifference and barbarity. Together, they embodied—though imperfectly—the risen Christ and became the vanguard for a new humanity.

At the same time, of course, all this was God's doing. To use Paul's language, as in the previous chapter, the first followers of Christ were what they were by the grace of God. They worked hard to be Christian and yet were always aware of the gifts they'd received. Their very lives and efforts were gifts, and they gave constant thanks and praise to God for what they had received.[11]

One occasion for thanksgiving and praise was the Sabbath, when routine and sweaty haste came to a stop, and the first Christians found time, together, for wonder and renewal. On Sabbath, work lost its power to oppress; monotony, its power to hypnotize. Now the first Christians could awake to a heightened sense of divine presence. They could hear the retelling of their story, adjust their lives accordingly, feel the darkness tremble when they joined together in one song. Now they could renew their watch-care over one another and find, in the friendship of the faithful, new energy for mission.

On Sabbath, in other words, they stopped so that the defining stories— of Abraham, of Moses and the prophets, of Jesus—could get under their skin and into their hearts and become once again *their* stories. They stopped so that, refreshed by rest and renewal, they could go forth in the peace of Christ to love and serve the wider world. They stopped so they could be, and remain, who they were: *disciples of Christ.*

It was the same when the first Christians broke bread. Often they did this together—one body, as Paul would say in 1 Corinthians, with many members. And again the story was central. You took food in the company of others, and then, in a much-repeated ritual, you heard how Jesus, on the night He was betrayed, washed the disciples' feet and afterward shared bread and wine with them. The breaking of the bread and pouring of the wine suggested His own soon-to-be-broken body; and, according to Matthew, this was a symbol of God's passion for forgiveness. The meal and the accompanying ritual told participants that despite adversity and suffering, they had reason to look backward with thanks and forward with hope.[12]

The first Christians felt called to live connected and illuminating lives and so to *be* the earthly embodiment of Christ. But if you took this to require flawlessness, it would be, of course, an impossible ideal. So from the start, Christians acknowledged that humans are flawed and goodness is fragile. But they also knew that when they fell short of goodness and hurt someone, or were hurt, they had one another for healing. This, too, was one meaning of the shared meal.

All the way back to Abraham, the Hebrew people had pursued daunting ideals. Now, under Jesus' influence, forgiveness had taken center stage. Practicing forgiveness was how the church would deal with human imperfection. The church would meet failure with forgiveness. It would meet even egregious failure—even violence—with forgiveness. That is how it would offer new life in the face of brokenness and keep alive the hope of reconciliation and renewal. Thus the church, though flawed, would embody God's point of view on earth.

It wasn't that forgiveness would be offered willy-nilly. In Matthew 18, you find Jesus putting forgiveness at the forefront. Yet in this chapter, He also envisions a disciple community in which people watch over and correct one another—and in which, for adamantly refusing to listen, an offender can even lose, at least for the time being, the privilege of membership. Paul said the same thing to the Corinthians. But as Matthew could envision repeated forgiveness—not seven times but seventy times seven—Paul could say, "Love never ends." In dealings with recalcitrant members, the point, always, is healing—healing of broken people, healing of the broken church. The point, always, is the "restoration of a rupture in the community."[13]

In Jesus' vision for all this, the watch-care involves conversation—two or three or more considering what to do in the face of disagreement. How do you reach, how do you learn from, how, if necessary, do you correct the offending person or group? Thus, when you refine your understanding of Christian life, the point is always *practical:* it is how you enhance—how you *improve*—the life and witness of the community.

According to Matthew 18, Jesus said that *He* would be present wherever "two or three" gather in His name. In John's account, Jesus promised that once His public ministry was over, He would be present to the disciples through the Holy Spirit. " 'I still have many things to say to you, but you cannot bear them now,' " He confided. Then He assured them that " 'when the Spirit of Truth comes, he will guide you into all the truth.' "[14] Through the ongoing presence of God, new understanding—a passion for improvement—would find support.

The practice of conversation, then, was like remembering the Sabbath or sharing the gospel meal. It was, by God's grace, another way of keeping the community strong; another way to resist dysfunction and strengthen resolve and assure that God's true colors can shine through.

In the Adventism that grew up in response to what Ellen White called the "primitive godliness" of the early church,[15] the Sabbath School came to be the occasion for this practice. Crisis or not, conversation would take place, and take place regularly. Being Adventist, after all, meant *becoming* Adventist—staying on the move, looking forward, always, to God's next transformation of shared life. Instead of feeling entirely at home with itself, the church would conduct a never-ending conversation based on the authority of the founding stories.[16] So it would guard against the ebbing of faithfulness. So it would make its journey, every week, into deeper understanding. And all the while it would observe this simple principle for interpreting the book that collects the founding stories: *Christ has the last word; you read the whole Bible in His light.*[17]

Thus it is that never, when you follow the New Testament way, do you burrow into sheer solitude. You practice community. You do so by participating in the *practices* that reinforce community. You and others are thus connected—like mountain climbers. And with the gift of shared strength, you become adventurous. You become adventurous enough to be an alternative to the commonplace, and even to be a revolution in the making.

Changing the World

In the year 390, Fabiola, a wealthy Christian woman from the city of Rome, helped invent a new institution. She'd been through a divorce, but she didn't hole up inside her wounded self, didn't let the pain define her life. Instead, she began attending to victims of disease and hunger in her city; victims the dominant pagan culture didn't really care about. Her teacher had been Saint Jerome. He said, "I have often seen her washing wounds which others—even men—could hardly bear to look at." In doing this, in giving "sufferers from the streets . . . all the attention of a nurse," she was founding—a hospital. She was offering care to ordinary

118

people, including the least of them, and was throwing herself into close connection with the sick.

Organizations focused on this kind of care for the sick hadn't existed before Christianity. Even the leading citizens of Rome lacked the right frame of mind, and emperors of the time, leaders among leading citizens, considered it their right to butcher and steal in order to expand and sustain imperial power. Pagans in general, both Roman and Greek, gave little attention to the vulnerable. In fact, they thought pity and mercy were pathological emotions. Plato, the brilliant philosopher, believed the best way to deal with beggars was to dump them outside the boundaries of the community.

The first Christians, building on Jewish ideals of hospitality, defied the heartlessness of the dominant culture. They cared about the poor as well as the rich, the unattractive as well as the good-looking, the powerless as well as the powerful. The hospitals that came into being with Fabiola and those who followed her drew circles large enough to include even people usually dismissed as undeserving. Together, these hospitals were a light—a beacon cutting through the dark. Today, institutions like this exist nearly everywhere. But as the medical historian Roy Porter declares, "Christianity planted the hospital"—or the kind of hospital, at least, where the spirit of Fabiola would prevail.[18]

Paul told the Corinthian Christians, "If anyone is in Christ, there is a new creation: everything old has passed away."[19] What he meant, it seems, is that a tiny filament of light can defy the darkness and bring new possibilities to view. A small number, even as few as one, can effect great change. So when a thoughtful few, joined to the church, cast off the jitters and begin to resist convention and to actually *be* the risen Christ on earth, the beauty of their holiness redeems the world.

Jesus had meant something like this when He told the disciples, " 'You are the salt of the earth' " and " 'the light of the world.' "[20] God's pioneers—the ones the book of Revelation calls the "remnant"[21]—would somehow break the stranglehold of evil. And when, after Luther, the Radical Reformers objected to "Christendom," or the idea of church and society as one, they were saying that the church is the company of the committed. You can't have a "Christian" nation or a "Christian" civilization in which the mere fact of your birth makes you a believer. You can only have volunteer Christians who have chosen to be baptized into Christ and whose old selves have been buried and new selves raised from the dead. Only then does the beloved community become a "lantern of righteousness" against the dark monotony of harm and hurt. Only then does it become a revolution in the making.[22]

Jews pioneered the idea of being a people who were "in but not of" the dominant, surrounding culture. It was always a costly experiment—a way of being that "required deep and unshakable conviction."[23] You had to have the courage to be different, to be the minority and not the majority. Jesus, Himself a Jew, exemplified it. And the first Christians knew that anyone who would belong to a lantern community, anyone who would be true salt and true light, must exemplify that courage too.

The reward of so doing is that *by being different you make a difference.* Along with others, you are the tiny filament of light that defies the darkness. You find yourself in league with Fabiola and the inventors of the hospital. Or, to bring in a recent witness, you identify with Martin Luther King, who in both spirit and power lived at the margin of American society, yet was the key to the civil rights revolution. Or you look with pride on the Adventist pioneers of better health, who, also from the American margin, have made an ever-stronger case for plant-based food and stimulated other forms of attention to bodily as well as spiritual well-being.

One twentieth-century giant among theologians with roots in the Radical Reformation was John Howard Yoder. "Social creativity," he wrote, "is a minority function." For him, the church was not only an alternative to business as usual, but also, by its example, a sign of hope and an architect of "restored humanity." In a sentence on the church as lovely and evocative as the dawn of day, he said, "The confessing people of God is the new world on its way."[24]

That is the ideal—or better, from a believer's standpoint, the reality: the beloved community *is* the new world on its way.

But when problems boil up in the church, how can this be plausible?

I have a friend who one day told my colleagues and me at the college where I work that hypocrisy "is bad, but the existence of hypocrisy is good." When we first heard this, we were puzzled. But we came to see the point. If your ideals are so low a troglodyte can reach them, that's hardly wonderful, hardly a reason to stand tall. It's like saying you have a moral vision and it's to stay out of jail or to stay sober before breakfast or to tell the truth for ten minutes. If you aspire to be way below average, you can say you're not a hypocrite, but so what?

When you think about it, you want ideals that stretch you so far you might not reach them. And from day one, that's been at the heart of the Hebrew response to God.

All the way back to Abraham, the Hebrew people have pursued daunting ideals, impossible dreams. A single family would bless all families? The church would be Christ on earth? A mere remnant would be a revolution in the making? Yes, that was the idea.

As in the case of the church at Corinth, life with this family, this remnant, was often underwhelming, disappointing, maddening. Still, the best people *believed*. It wasn't optimism that kept them going; it was *faith*. All that was good was God's. Their hope, however outlandish, was good, and like every ounce of effort they put in and like their very lives, it was God's: God's dream. God's gift. God's work.

The divine patience somehow reinforced this sense of things. As underwhelming, disappointing, and maddening as the church might be, God wouldn't give up on those who comprised it. God was always ready to open another door to yet another beginning. And if God didn't give up on them, they wouldn't give up on God.

That patience, that readiness to forgive, came not only to define the idea of God, but also to define the ideal response to God. Saying Yes to God meant saying Yes to the people God had made. With Jesus, this sensibility took center stage. As God didn't give up on you, you didn't give up on others. Meeting failure with forgiveness was the way to deal with human imperfection.

That is why the faults of the beloved community do not doom its revolutionary project. It remains, though imperfectly, the embodiment of divine forgiveness, and just for this reason it can provide, despite the

The Promise of Peace

faults, a "facilitating environment"—a framework, in other words, for the development of trust and moral sensitivity.[25] It can provide enough support, enough patience, and enough hope to nourish and sustain a Fabiola, a Martin Luther King, a band of health researchers at Loma Linda University.

What is more, the beloved community can provide enough of these to nourish and sustain *us,* and, by its shared practices and outlandish hope, embolden *us* to live our best and deepest dreams, and actually to *be,* by God's grace, a revolution in the making.

---

1. For the problems, see the first few chapters of Paul's first letter to the Corinthians. In his first chapter, though, he can say that the Corinthian members have been called to shame the "strong" and "reduce to nothing things that are" (verses 27, 28). A few lines down (2:8)—and here is a clue to what he means by the "things that are"—he speaks of the "rulers of this age," who have "crucified the Lord of glory."

2. Quoted in Richard Hays, *First Corinthians,* Interpreter's Bible Commentary (Louisville, Ky.: John Knox Press, 1997), 66. On pagan religious experience and philosophical alternatives in the context of a moral crisis, see Rodney Stark, *The Rise of Christianity* (Princeton, N.J.: Princeton University Press, 1996), 79–94.

3. 1 Corinthians 1:23, 24 and 6:9–11.

4. 2 Corinthians 5:18–20. The church's "mission," writes Adventist theologian Gottfried Oosterwal, is to "participate in God's own mission." See his *Mission: Possible* (Nashville: Southern Publishing Association, 1972), 69.

5. Acts 1:8.

6. Acts 2:46.

7. See Romans 6:1–4.

8. See, e.g., Romans 12:19 and 1 John 2:7.

9. Margaret Edson, *Wit* (New York: Faber and Faber, 1999), 66.

10. Richard Rice, *Believing, Behaving, Belonging: Finding New Love for the Church* (Roseville, Calif.: Association of Adventist Forums, 2002), 115, 120.

11. See 1 Corinthians 15:9, 10, 57; see, too, chapter 12 for the sense of Christian life as a gift.

12. On the church as the body of Christ, see 1 Corinthians 12, especially verse 27. On footwashing, see John 13:1–12. For Paul's account of what came to be called the Lord's Supper, see 1 Corinthians 11:23–33; for Matthew's, see Matthew 26:26–30.

13. I rely for this last phrase and substantially in the whole paragraph on James Wm. McClendon Jr., *Ethics: Systematic Theology,* 2d ed., vol. 1 (Nashville: Abingdon, 2002), 225–227. I allude to, or quote passages from Matthew 18, 1 Corinthians 5 and 6, and, for the comment on love, 1 Corinthians 13:8.

14. Matthew 18:20; John 16:12, 13.

15. In *The Great Controversy,* 464. Ellen White associated such godliness with "apostolic times." What happened *then* provided guidance for what happens *now.*

16. James Wm. McClendon speaks, from his Radical Reformation perspective, of "never-ending congregational *conversation.*" McClendon, 225.

17. See, e.g., Hebrews 4:1–3, the single best New Testament passage on how to read the Bible.

18. For the story and the final quote, see Roy Porter, *The Greatest Benefit to Mankind: A Medical History of Humanity* (New York: Norton, 1998), 88. *See also* Roy Porter, *Blood Guts: A Short History of Medicine* (London: Norton, 2002), 135, where the author allows that imperial Rome provided some hospital facilities, but not for "the civilian sick." Hospitals predating Christianity, in Sri Lanka and India, tended toward the isolation of, as opposed to intimate care of, the patient, a point made in the online version of the *Encyclopaedia Britannica,* http://www.britannica.com/EBchecked/topic/272626/hospital. Accessed March 16, 2009. For the account of pagan sensibility, I depend also on Rodney Stark, *The Rise of Christianity: A Sociologist Reconsiders History* (Princeton, N.J.: Princeton University Press, 1996), 212.

19. 2 Corinthians 5:17.

20. Matthew 5:13, 14.

21. Revelation 12:17, KJV.

22. The "lantern" metaphor is from the Anabaptist Balthasar Hubmaier and is quoted in Walter Klaassen, ed., *Anabaptism in Outline: Selected Primary Sources* (Scottdale, Penn.: Herald Press, 1981), 102.

23. James Wm. McClendon Jr., *Doctrine: Systematic Theology,* vol. 2 (Nashville: Abingdon, 1994), 356.

24. John Howard Yoder, *The Royal Priesthood: Essays Ecclesiological and Ecumenical* (Scottdale, Penn.: Herald Press, 1998), 315, 373. The words on social creativity are reminiscent of a famous quote—hard to pin down; it may be from a newspaper interview—attributed to anthropologist Margaret Mead: "Never doubt that a small group of thoughtful, committed citizens can change the world. Indeed, it is the only thing that ever has."

25. The quoted phrase appears in remarks on infancy by the pediatrician Donald Winnicott. See Martha Nussbaum's discussion of Winnicott in *Upheavals of Thought: The Intelligence of Emotions* (Cambridge: Cambridge University Press, 2001), 185, 186, 224–229.

10

Engaging the Other

You meet others every day.

Some look and sound the way you do. They're "your people." Some are different. They wear baseball caps at weird angles, and you don't. They eat fried okra, and you eat mashed potatoes. They talk fancy, and you talk plain. They're richer than you are, or poorer.

The differences may involve conviction—life-shaping belief. Some people are Catholic, and you're Pentecostal. Some vote for one political party, you vote for another. Some go on and on about injustice and wink at infidelity; others dwell on personal values and hard work and accept a society of haves and have-nots.

Now and then you meet people—on television, or, these days, right where you live and work—who are *really* different. They have an entirely different religion from yours. They grow long beards or cover their hair and faces or shave their heads and wear long robes and live apart from the hurly-burly in communities of meditation.

Some people, you learn, eat the flesh of animals that you thought were household pets or believe in genital mutilation of girls or train children to blow themselves up for a cause. To people whose perspective differs from yours, it may be just as shocking that you give the elderly so little honor, or consume so much of the world's resources, or drive around with the top down dressed in a bikini.

Variety is a fact. The dark side of variety is reckless passion for what "my people"—the people I know and identify with—think best. All too often, this passion churns into violence, leaving a ruin of broken hearts and dreams. Think Bosnia and the Congo, Northern Ireland and the Middle East; think Rwanda, Sri Lanka, and the Sudan. Or consider the long history of racial discord in America and elsewhere around the world. Recall, too, the World Trade Center and the long and violent hatreds of which it is a symbol. The places are familiar, and the list, lengthy.

One solution, widely put forward, is tolerance. In being tolerant, you respect people who see things differently from you by keeping your convictions to yourself. At the least, you don't try to change or "convert" people. This is a fashionable ideal and a close cousin to relativism—the view that how people interpret the world reflects, or is related to, how and where they have grown up. Relativism says that everyone looks through the lens of his or her own culture. Everyone sees from an angle, has a limited perspective, knows only part of what can be known. Grow up on America's urban streets, and you perceive one world. Grow up in the suburbs, or in Baghdad, and you perceive another. And since no one has the God's-eye view, no one can claim—so says extreme relativism— to know more about the truth than others know.

Both tolerance and relativism work best or seem most acceptable when people are prosperous and happy. In difficult times, it is natural to assign blame, or even to look for scapegoats. Then even the well-educated may turn on the strangers they have heretofore put up with and kept at arm's length. Our parents and grandparents were alive when Germany, then the best-educated country in Europe, skidded into ever-deeper resentment and self-doubt and in the end turned its murderous rage against the Jews. We all know that smart, well-educated people commit acts of war and terror.[1]

One poet speaks of "the basic similarity of humans / And their tiny grain of dissimilarity."[2] Both are wonderful. Similarity unites. Dissimilarity adds interest as to food and song and dress. But it may also set minds on edge, make voices shrill, goad people into savage acts.

That is why encounter with others is no matter of indifference. When you meet someone, especially someone who is a stranger, you hold the future in your hands. Whether you enhance that future or debase it depends on how you feel, think, and act. And the Christian responsibility for these interactions cannot be overstated. Religion has growing influence worldwide, though perhaps less so in the most developed countries. Among the world's religions, Christianity—so one authority declares—will leave on the twenty-first century the deepest mark of all.[3]

What will that mark be?

Learning From Others

A man dressed as a clown appeared at the trial of a Frenchman who, now an old man, was charged with deporting Jews to Germany during World War II. The defendant was said to have done this during the period when the French government was cooperating with Hitler. That was a time when Jews who ended up in Germany typically met with death. After the war, the defendant had escaped notice and risen to a high position in government.

The clown suit was the spectator's expression of outrage; it dramatized the absurdity of what had happened. When he was barred from entering the courtroom, he came back in street dress and attended the remainder of the trial. The day the guilty verdict was finally announced, a court attendant heard him say, "Without truth, how can there be hope?"[4]

In a many-cultured world, how can the question of truth—of what's the case and what's not, what's right and what's wrong—come into play? After all, even the apostle Paul said that we know only in part. He knew that we each perceive the world through glasses that limit the view.[5] So, how can exchanges between people with different backgrounds help? How can conversation build hope for humanity instead of worry and despair? What is the alternative to endless disagreement and recurring violence?

According to the Bible, God addressed human brokenness by challenging a man and his family to become repairers of that brokenness. Abraham and his seed, God declared, would be the bearers of blessing for all—the first peacemakers. The Hebrew people who came out of Abraham's experience had no interest, it turned out, in abstract truth, no interest in knowledge for its own sake. But they did have a passion for saving truth, for knowledge applied to human need and aimed at the healing of human relationships. Without saving truth, there could be no hope.

At the point when God said "all the families of the earth" would be "blessed" through Abraham, the first word was "Go." "Now the LORD said to Abram, 'Go from your country and your kindred and your father's house.' "[6] It was in the going—in the long journey to a world of strangers—that Abraham and his seed would become the first peacemakers.

In other words, connecting with people who are different would be the daily lot of the Hebrew people. They would be strangers themselves, and would, as God said another time, love the strangers they met.[7] In crossing borders, they would bear the blessing. Instead of merely tolerating others, they would interact with them.

One of the best border-crossing stories to emerge from this legacy concerns Jesus' entrance into the region of Tyre and Sidon. The story shows the difficulty of truthful encounter with another, and it shows the rewards that follow effort, even halting effort.

Strangers abounded in Tyre and Sidon and its surroundings. The Greek-speaking city dwellers looked down on the Jewish farmers in the countryside, and the Jewish farmers looked down on the city dwellers. Ethnic tension bristled. When Jesus arrived, He had already collected followers and established a ministry of teaching and healing. But He had also begun to sense the danger in His mission. Herod, the puppet governor, had executed John the Baptist, a man whose vision Jesus largely shared. That execution was ominous.

Feeling the strain, Jesus entered a house, hoping, so Mark tells us, that no one would know He was there.[8] But a woman found Him. This was in itself remarkable. Women then had no right to assert themselves. And what is more, this woman belonged to a culture and an ethnic group the Jews had little time for.

But she knew the reputation Jesus had for healing, and her daughter was desperately ill. So, prostrating herself, she begged for healing mercy. According to Matthew, however, Jesus ignored her. And when the disciples, who considered her a pest, urged Him to "send her away," Jesus responded with apparent sympathy for their point of view: " 'I was sent only to the lost sheep of the house of Israel.' " At this moment it seemed clear that she was outside the circle of His concern.

In Matthew's telling of the story, that's how Jesus saw His mission, and that's why He was ignoring the woman's supplications: she was a Canaanite, outside of the house of Israel. When the woman persisted, Jesus dismissed her. " 'It is not fair to take the children's food and throw it to the dogs,' " He said. It was a pointed ethnic reference and must have hurt her feelings.

During His boyhood, Jesus had sat long hours listening to the rabbis and asking questions. He had been eager to learn, and all the while He had "increased in wisdom . . . , and in divine and human favor."[9] Now, meeting a stranger who refused to be docile, Jesus was about to take another step in the journey that He had begun while He was still a child. The woman, hearing His sharp words, made a jaw-dropping rejoinder.

Remember that for Canaanites, unlike the Jews of that day, dogs could be pets: they were not unclean and not excluded. Around the table that this woman knew, even the dogs ate. So, bending Jesus' words to her own purpose, she said, " 'Yes, Lord, yet even the dogs eat the crumbs that fall from their masters' table.' "

According to Matthew, these words *made a difference for Jesus.* From that point forward, His emphasis shifted. Not only did He heal the woman's daughter, but He also became more intentional about the Gentiles. Now for the first time He began reaching out to Gentile *crowds.*[10]

Jesus did *not* make a practice of always suspending judgment. That may be the fashion when mere tolerance is the ideal and you learn not to judge other persons or other cultures. But Jesus had a mission to change minds. He *did* make judgments about others and *did* invite them to consider the point of view He stood for. At the same time, however, He was able to break out of His own skin and learn—learn from a stranger's point of view.

The Gospel account shows Jesus *engaging the other,* taking the person different from Himself *seriously.* But if it shows Jesus seeing with other eyes and feeling with another's heart, it doesn't say that crossing borders is easy. The story shows the difficulty encounter with strangers may involve. Still, what it mainly shows is the value of a stranger's assertiveness against our natural resistance to larger vision.

When you meet another person who engages you in life-changing conversation, you meet a gift from God. The Canaanite woman was such a gift to Jesus.[11]

Bearing Witness

All this suggests a standard for being human in a world of difference. It is *self-confidence enhanced by humility.* You have a point of view, and you embrace it with passion. You undertake a mission, and you pursue it with passion. But your passion is not the reckless vehemence that says "my people" know it all; it's not the wanton self-regard that veers to the edge, or over the edge, of violence.

The passion proper to the border-crossing legacy tries to look with other eyes and feel with other hearts. It takes a position and works for a goal but is neither self-sufficient nor self-satisfied. It is eager to find seeds for new vision and new being in the challenge of another person's face, another person's point of view.[12]

When you are faithful to the way of Jesus, you see life among the many cultures as an opportunity. However difficult it may be, you reach out, not only to friends but also to strangers, listening and learning as well as sharing and persuading. You acknowledge the Canaanite woman—the seeker, the antagonist—and let that person's life and words undermine complacency and summon you to growth. Again and again you and those with whom you share the Christian life seize the gift of new understanding. Again and again you find, through conversation, a more faithful way of being the person, and the people, you are called to be.

But it's not only that you listen, you also share your viewpoint. At the right moment you even confront and challenge those who disagree with you. Paul, the first and foremost of Christian missionaries, acknowledged that human beings can see and know only in part. He agreed, though he didn't use these words, that a *soft* version of relativism is true: we do perceive things from an angle, and we do have a limited perspective. But he *still* bore a witness. He didn't throw up his hands and say, as in *extreme* relativism, that everyone is boxed into an inherited point of view and the search for truth is pointless. Instead, he changed his mind himself and asked others to change theirs. When you do as he did—stand up for saving truth, like Jesus and the Hebrew prophets—you cannot be so polite that you never raise a question or make a protest. But neither, of course, can you be so proud that you never have doubt or look to others, even strangers, for deeper understanding.

Witness is not indifference. Witness is not arrogance. The chart below shows the range of attitudes and habits—virtues or vices—that help define the person who, in a many-cultured world, truly becomes a witness.

Indifference	Witness	Arrogance
• Apathy	• Passion	• Fanaticism
• Wishy-washiness	• Conviction	• Smugness
• Self-reproach	• Humility	• Conceit
• Obsequiousness	• Respect	• Contempt
• Tolerance	• Conversation	• Intolerance
• Vacillation	• Openness to change	• Rigidity
• Reticence	• Advocacy	• Violence

Engaging the other, and doing so with integrity, is never easy or automatic. But without this integrity—without *witness*—there can be no authentic quest for truth. And as the man with the clown suit suggested, without truth there can be no hope.

These days the borders that give rise to strangeness and make us so

130

aware of strangers are both obvious and daunting. But when you become part of the story told in Scripture, crossing those borders is how you live. Through reading and other media, and through personal interactions, you *connect* with strangers as well as friends. You make the journey of Abraham.

Along the way—the Christian way—you take your cues, most importantly, from Jesus. The biblical story, with its climax in the "Father, forgive them" of the cross[13] and the joyous turnaround of resurrection, gives strength and guidance every day. You adjust as conversation casts new light upon the path. You pray never to drift with the wind of fashion, never to bend to the will of those with stony hearts and paltry sympathies. Blessing for all is the grand and inviolate ideal. The way of Jesus is the means to its realization; it is how the ideal comes to be on earth as it is in heaven.[14]

In crossing borders, determination to stay true to the best in your heritage must match the courage it takes to be open to new understanding. Following the Resurrection, Paul broke a path to the Gentiles, and the blessing God had promised Abraham spread across the world as it never had before. Paul and generations after him encountered pagan others—others marked by the sins and sway of Rome. In their conversation with these others, they sought to understand them and to share their own understanding, and they invited them to join their congregations. Christian generosity was more inclusive than what the pagans knew, and many found that generosity compelling.

Under the impact of the wider witness that Paul began, the church advanced in numbers and in influence.[15] But it also took a catastrophic turn. Despite Paul's reminder that the seed of Abraham is "the root that supports you,"[16] the church pulled away from the Hebrew people, abandoning the Sabbath and diminishing the affirmation of the body and the earth that was part of its heritage from Judaism. Christian interest in the joys and tasks of earthly life shriveled, and the comprehensive hope of Scripture became a largely otherworldly fixation.

What is more, the church began drifting into partnership with Rome. Even though Jesus had refused to cozy up to Herod, forgetful Christian leaders allowed their community to take on the trappings and attitude of the empire. This further eviscerated Christian witness. The church became, more often than not, an unholy echo of political establishments, whether imperial, democratic, fascist, or otherwise.

Knowledge wrung from darkness, it turns out, is darkness still.

If witness in a many-cultured world opens doors to deeper understanding, it may also, if undisciplined, shut doors to wider peace. The danger exemplified in the church's compromise with Rome remains. Reckless change is as dangerous as smug self-satisfaction. In their different ways, both fall short of the standard—self-confidence in league with humility—and both imperil the inviolate ideal and defining way of Israel's God.

So, if encounter with others makes authentic witness possible, it also puts that witness gravely at risk. But the risk was there at the beginning, when Abraham left the security of the familiar for the adventure of mission. When you are Christian and you embrace the border-crossing legacy, you run the risk. But you also pray—not just for the courage to change but also for deliverance from thoughtless drift into something less than the will and way of Christ.

And all along, you live from the hope that springs eternal by the grace of God. It is the hope that keeps you focused on the day when belligerence and isolation will cease, and the dark side of variety in human affairs will give way to the winsomeness of peace, and a single "pulse of harmony and gladness" will beat "through the vast creation."[17]

When things go right, that is where authentic reaching out to others takes us.

---

1. See, in Theodore Zeldin, *An Intimate History of Humanity* (New York: Harper Perennial, 1996), the chapter on "Why Toleration Has Never Been Enough," 256–273.

2. As Czeslaw Milosz does in his poem, "Eyes," in *The New Yorker,* August 19 and 26, 2002, 76.

3. See Philip Jenkins, "The Next Christianity," in *The Atlantic,* October 2002, 53–68; *See also* his *The Next Christendom: The Coming of Global Christianity* (New York:

Oxford University Press, 2002).

4. The incident, which involved the author's real-life father, became the basis for Michel Quint's work of fiction, *In Our Strange Gardens,* reviewed by Richard Eder, "A Clown Whose Message Is No Laughing Matter," *New York Times,* December 7, 2001, E39.

5. 1 Corinthians 13:12.

6. Genesis 12:1–3.

7. Deuteronomy 10:19.

8. Mark's account appears in 7:24–30; Matthew's in his Gospel, 15:21–28.

9. Luke 2:46, 52.

10. Matthew's account, on which I have mainly relied, is in 15:21–28. Besides commentaries, I have consulted Judith Gundry-Volf, "Spirit, Mercy and the Other," in *Theology Today* 52 (1 1995): 508–522.

11. For a literary reflection on the value of the other, consider C. S. Lewis, *An Experiment in Criticism* (Cambridge: Cambridge University Press, 1969 [copyrighted 1961]). What Lewis says about reading has affected how I think about conversation with others. "The necessary condition of all good reading is 'to get ourselves out of the way,' " and to seek the enlargement of "mental being," not just the enlargement of "self-esteem." These quotes are from pages 93 and 115.

12. My language here reflects Emmanuel Levinas, on whom Michael Barnes, *Theology and the Dialogue of Religions* (Cambridge: Cambridge University Press, 2002), has written helpfully.

13. Luke 23:34.

14. As for the centrality of Jesus, this is what John teaches when, in 16:12–15, he says the disciples will learn many things they cannot now bear, and says, too, that the Spirit who guides them will always "glorify" Jesus.

15. An arresting account of this growth is found in Rodney Stark, *The Rise of Christianity: A Sociologist Reconsiders History* (Princeton: Princeton University Press, 1996). Stark argues that the steady growth reflected superior moral vision and the prospect, for converts, of benefits they could not otherwise receive.

16. Romans 11:18.

17. Ellen White, *The Great Controversy,* 678.

11

Growing the Church

When I was an eighth-grader in Spokane, a visiting evangelist opened his meetings with a sermon called "Blood and Snow on the Hills of Washington." The sermons that followed, in a former auto dealership rigged up with platform and chairs, were equally compelling. And as the weeks of meetings went by, the evangelist attempted to build up Adventism by tearing down its competitors. His self-assurance was, to me, riveting. The whole spectacle—the dark hall, the spotlight, the white jacket and golden hair—was as vivid as a poster.

The evangelist singled out Roman Catholics in particular when he spoke one Sunday night on "The Mark of the Beast." Spokane was strongly Catholic, and during the week that followed, rumors about anger and possible threats against the evangelist began to surface among the Adventists in town. The next Sunday night the topic was "The Antichrist." Everyone wondered how it would go. I was amazed, when I got there, to see police officers in the hall, standing to each side, peering into the crowd.

No tempers flared, however, and we Adventists left the hall relieved and newly assured of our own worth, our own superiority. That was a long time ago. Now the mere telling of the story evokes discomfort.

But not, perhaps, for everyone. People still listen to preaching, Adventist and otherwise, that harks back to what I heard as a boy. The preachers' preoccupations may resemble or differ from the ones I recall, but evangelism still seems, all too often, prideful to the point of arrogance. And for many today, this is not just embarrassing, it's contemptible.

Tony Campolo, the Baptist professor-preacher, makes the point about how widespread this feeling is when he explains the way he handles seatmates on long plane rides. If someone asks him what he does and Campolo *wants* to talk, he says, "I'm a sociologist," and more questions follow. If he's asked the question and he *doesn't* want to talk, he just says, "I'm a Baptist evangelist." Most of the time, that's a conversation stopper.

But Jesus did say, " 'Go . . . and make disciples of all nations, baptizing them in the name of the Father and of the Son and of the Holy Spirit, and teaching them to obey everything that I have commanded you.' "[1] And in the book of Acts, Luke did describe a growing church and a passion among its leaders for evangelism. The first Christians took their case for the gospel into the synagogues and marketplaces. When they began, they were a faction within Judaism, but it wasn't long until Peter had founded a mission to the Gentiles. Soon Paul was invoking Isaiah's vision of "light for the Gentiles" reaching to "the ends of the earth," and he was traveling farther and farther from Jerusalem with his message about the resurrected Jesus.[2]

The Christian interpretation of Abraham's heritage began getting attention from leaders of the paganism then dominant in the Roman Empire. As church membership grew, competition intensified, with each side making its arguments and responding to ever-sharper counter-arguments. Over time, however, Christian ideas just seemed better, and the pagan ramparts began to weaken.

The church's swift expansion had, it's true, a downside. I noted in the previous chapter and also in chapter 3 that as pagan ideas were being challenged, they were also seeping in, some to the gospel's detriment, and the church found itself compromised as well as increasingly successful. Down the years, awareness of compromise would sharpen the definite, if still developing, sense of the church's need for *continual self-criticism.* But for our purposes now, the point is that the first Christians were going forth to make new disciples.

The new movement's progress was steady, if not overwhelming. By the year 100—long after Paul and other pioneers were gone—the total number of Christians in the world amounted, by one estimate, to about seventy-five hundred. Still, early adopters were embracing the new faith. They were dissatisfied with conventional ways, and they told their stories to their friends and acquaintances. The new vision, still tied to its Jewish roots and still attractive to many Jews, spread from one social network to another, reaching the educated and the well-off as well as the uneducated and the poor. After three centuries or so, Christianity had become a cultural innovation no thoughtful person could ignore.[3]

Twice in that early period a plague swept through the Roman Empire, taking as many as 30 percent of the people to an early death. Both times the Christian community stood out for being different. During the first epidemic, starting around 165 c.e., Galen was the most famous physician alive. He served Marcus Aurelius, the Roman emperor, and his writing about medicine was earning respect that would last for centuries. But Galen was pagan at a time when the Jesus movement had not yet upended the pagan understanding of human value and human purposes. So as the danger mounted, it made sense to him, despite the thousands who needed treatment, to decamp from Rome to a safe retreat in Asia Minor.

Meanwhile, Christians stayed by the epidemic's victims. They nursed one another and nursed their pagan neighbors. Their own safety was in jeopardy, but they persisted and saved many lives. The new morality—of kindness for all; of regard for neighbor equal to regard for self—had taken hold and was having an effect.

A hundred years later, when the second plague came, the difference between the pagan and the Christian frame of mind again was evident. Dionysius, leader of the church in Alexandria, said many of his members lost their lives for braving the dangers of compassion. His tribute to them evoked Jesus Himself: in "nursing" others, he said, they had "transferred their death to themselves and died in their stead."

Constantine had embraced Christianity near the beginning of the fourth century, but less than twenty-five years after his demise, a pagan emperor named Julian ascended to power. With defections to the Christian side continuing to mount, Julian complained that they were due largely to Christian "benevolence toward strangers." Christians cared for their own needy and "for ours as well," he told one priest in exasperation. Wanting to restore paganism to its former prominence, Julian urged pagan priests to match what Christians were doing for their neighbors. But the response was paltry. There were no pagan ideas—no pagan teachings or traditions—for the priests to build upon. No pagan thought that God loves us or that because God loves us we must love one another. No pagan thought of mercy as an ideal—to say nothing of thinking that it should extend beyond family and tribe to the outsider and even the enemy.[4]

Christian ideas stood out in other ways as well. While the pagan world was rife with gloom and with contempt for human flesh and human circumstances, Christianity promised newness of life and the resurrection of the flesh. In the pagan culture, women suffered from mistreatment and no one bothered to condemn it; the drowning of unwanted children seemed reasonable even to philosophers; and urban life was brutal and chaotic, especially for the poor. The church, on the other hand, was giving new power and freedom to women; it was saying an emphatic No to infanticide; and it was offering stable and wholesome relationships to otherwise lonely people. In all these ways, the followers of Jesus came across as a "revitalization movement." The church's new perspective was providing new norms, new solidarity, and new hope.[5]

To echo words from a previous chapter, during these early years the church seemed actually to *be* the new world on its way. And in that light the church could and did make a case for the gospel. It could and did recruit others to discipleship. It really was an evangelistic community.

Embarrassment or Thing of Beauty?

"And how are they to believe in one of whom they have never heard?" Paul put this question to the Christians in Rome. Then he added, "And how are they to hear without someone to proclaim him?"

The Promise of Peace

You can't benefit, or benefit fully, from someone you know nothing about. So to Paul, for whom Christ was the key to human flourishing, a mission of evangelism was as indispensable—and as winsome—as light. It was natural for him, in the same passage of his letter to the Romans, to invoke the Hebrew prophet who exclaimed, "How beautiful upon the mountains are the feet of the messenger who announces peace" and "brings good news."[6]

Identifying with all this, some say evangelism is why the church exists. Telling the story, saying the words—that's the whole point. Anything else matters less, or is even a distraction. But just for the reasons that explain why paganism stumbled, this is a mistake. Words can be propaganda. Words can be a huckster's low-down manipulation. And in any case, it wasn't a message, or mere words, that broke paganism's hold. It was a way of life. What got everyone's attention was the church's passion to *be* the presence of Christ in the world. What so befuddled the defenders of the old way was the unassailable argument of love—love embodied in family relationships, love reaching out to strangers, love put to work in the midst of danger.

Jesus said God's true children make peace. They don't hurt others; they heal and restore. They don't resign themselves to what is; they commit themselves to what could be. In the spirit of God's "covenant of peace," they live for the prosperity and well-being of all. God's mission is their mission.[7]

But if the goal is peace and the means is love, words do matter. Julian found out that you can't just *decree* generosity. A generous heart requires the lifeblood of empowering conviction. With nothing but contempt for human flesh and human circumstances, you will be a prisoner of hopelessness and find little reason to transcend self-preoccupation. But with a sense that the world is hospitable to generosity, you may hearken to the better voices that address you.

A witness of words cannot be the whole of Christian mission. But the mission does require the message. You have to tell a convincing story. You have to make a case. You have to win—let me say this plainly—you have to *win* converts, and you have to *keep* them.

138

For some good reasons and some bad, this offends contemporary sensibility. To many, these days, proselytism, or the practice of making converts, is blustery and fraudulent. In part, this is because persuasion itself, perhaps more than ever, comes across as suspect—as nothing but a ploy for power. Swindlers and tyrants attempt to change people's minds, and everyone knows they are manipulators. They use words as weapons. Trying to impose their perspective on truth, they advance themselves at the expense of others. In their different ways, swindlers and tyrants alike are pitiless and violent.

Harsh judgments against Christian evangelism reflect these misgivings about persuasion. They reflect, too, dark turns in the actual history of the church. When Constantine allied himself with the new faith (and made its God into a God of war), he legalized the worship of Christ and established religious liberty for Christians. But he was soon restricting the right of Jews to make converts to their religion. Not long after Constantine, Augustine, the most influential bishop of his age, was arguing for use of force in defense of orthodox faith. By some six centuries later, Pope Urban II was calling Christians into battle against Islam, which then controlled Jerusalem. This would be a "pilgrim's war," said the pope, and he promised that those who fought in it would receive "immediate forgiveness for their sins" and so be assured of an eternal afterlife.[8]

Historians later named this assault the First Crusade. Religious coercion led up to it, and religious coercion followed, becoming practically routine. Once the Roman Empire had splintered into smaller states, wars *between* Christians, fought in God's name, became a staple of the European experience. It is little wonder, then, that Christian persuasion—in the form, sometimes, of the badly named evangelistic "crusade"—now seems dubious or even dangerous.

Even among Christians, enthusiasm for making new disciples has diminished. On hearing about his mother's plans for an overseas "mission trip," a young man I know asked, "Why do we think we know what's best for other countries?" Once, at the prospect of an evangelistic initiative by the congregation I was leading, a nervous member said, "I just wish we never tried to get anyone to join our church."

I suppose that for negative feeling about church growth, you couldn't top this last remark. But you *can* explain it. Thoughtful people see good things in more than one religion or philosophy. Thoughtful people know the church's startling imperfections. Thoughtful people recognize that no human point of view is free from bias and self-interest. So, to many of them, it seems best for people considering life's big questions to rely on their own reasoning power and make their decisions for themselves. The church's witness of words seems intrusive. They distrust and resent people who want to change other people's minds.

From the Bible's standpoint, of course, Christian existence is always a missionary existence. You possess what God gives so that you may impart it to others. Still, the objections to a missionary existence are forceful, and they deserve careful consideration. What can be said about these objections that might also be forceful? And can you say it in the spirit of the Christ you are called to proclaim?

Peaceable Witness

In "Dreamer," the heavy metal superstar Ozzy Osbourne says he wishes we could "live as one"—without "each other's help there ain't no hope for us." As for the "higher power" you honor and uphold, that "doesn't really matter much to me." But something that *does* matter to Ozzy Osbourne is whether you try to *convince others* concerning what you believe. As he makes clear in "Under the Sun," Ozzy Osbourne is uncomfortable with advocates. He doesn't want a "Jesus freak" or "preacher" or anyone else telling him "what to do. / I just believe in myself / 'cause no one else is true."[9]

It's the spirit of the age—or the so-called "new age"—to think that you may shop around among many sources for whatever help you want, and then, out of what you find, build a *personal* philosophy of life. There is no good reason to belong to a specific community—no good reason to be a Christian, say, as opposed to something else. But the truth is that high risk accompanies this line of reasoning, and you will see it as soon as you stop to think. Consider a cartoon I once saw. An air traffic controller, the picture of nonchalance, is leaning back in his chair, legs crossed at the ankles, and feet resting on his desk. Responding to the pilot of an incoming aircraft, he says, "I don't know. What do *you* want to do?"

Sometimes, surely, a case has to be made. Who, after all, would stand by in amiable silence when confronted with the gas chambers? Or with the genital mutilation of young girls? Or with suicide bombings? And who would ask Martin Luther King, the prophet of racial equality, to please keep out of other people's business?

Some would, I suppose. The indifferent are many. So are those who bristle when reformers raise their voices. And if you want a world where bullies have their way, you can be like them. But as soon as you aim for human harmony and make the care and keeping of one another into an ideal, you must *object* when some organization, or some individual, runs roughshod over other people. If the offending organization—a rogue government, a corrupt business, a gang of drug dealers—doesn't want some "Jesus freak" or "preacher" telling it what to do, you must express your outrage nonetheless. And if the offending individual puts up a defense by claiming the right to "believe in myself / 'cause no one else is true," you must simply say, "That's not your right at all. You are deluded."

A famous rabbi said, "To be is to stand for."[10] Now the question is: How can you stand for something responsibly? How can you bear an authentic—not a manipulative—witness of words? How can you proclaim the gospel in a way that reflects the spirit of the Christ who is its subject?

As we saw in the previous chapter, when you interact with someone different from you, the most helpful frame of mind is self-confidence enhanced by humility. This means, first, that you listen. You may want someone to come over to your point of view, and you may be justified in making that attempt—but not if you think you already know all you need to know. If you take no interest in what another person has to say, making your case *is* objectionable. You won't learn anything about the other person's hopes and fears. You won't hear anything that puts your own convictions in a fresh, or even unsettling, perspective. In short, you won't so much *love* the other person as *use* that person to advance your own interests. Unless witness is conversation, it's just another name for arrogance.

The good witness opens up to the other person (or other culture or religion). But if you are mature in this way, you also, as a good witness, *make your case.* The first Christians lived where it was easy to be numbed into compliance with business as usual. Pagan cults were everywhere. Caesar's image was on the coins in practically every town, and you couldn't miss the suggestion that he was worthy of worship. Many, indeed, thought that Caesar was himself a manifestation of God. But against the pagan monopoly on human imagination, the New Testament held up the risen Christ. As the Letter to the Colossians said, He alone is "the image of the invisible God." Others may want to make you "captive" to a different philosophy or vision, but you should resist them: Christ is "the head over every power and authority."[11]

In New Testament perspective, then, every Christian *has a case to make.* Not every religion or philosophy is equally devoted to good things. The gospel is different, and the gospel is better. So once you have embraced it, you proclaim it. You highlight what's distinctive. You draw out the pertinent contrasts. In the end, you invite people to embrace it themselves—you invite them into the beloved community.

But now a heart-stopping reminder, also from the Letter to the Colossians: "And let the peace of Christ rule in your hearts."

People who *stand* for something slip easily into arrogance and manipulation. So the thing to remember, and remember fiercely, is that no witness is fully Christian unless it is peaceable. In making a case to others, as in every facet of the Christian life, the ideal is "the way of peace," for which, as Luke said, Jesus is our standard and our guide.[12] True witness, therefore, responds to the needs of the other. True witness is patient and kind and doesn't insist on its own way. True witness bears pain without passing it on; it does no violence even to its enemies. True witness has a single passion, and that is the flourishing of all—the divine will done on earth as it is in heaven.

The gospel reimagines the world. Against ordinary inclination, it says that the everyday powers that be, with all their might and money, have no final say-so: Christ is sovereign over every one of them—over "every power and authority."

If this reimagined world is to be plausible at all, those who bear witness to it must be flesh-and-blood signs of its reality. Words matter, but words alone are flimflam. In the competition among religions and philosophies, it is *lives* that really make the case. And for the gospel, the lives that matter are the ones that reflect Christ's sovereignty—the ones that show, even if imperfectly, the sheer beauty of the Christian way.

James and Isabella Howard, both African Americans and both new to Adventism, were among the twenty-six charter members of the first Seventh-day Adventist Church to organize in Washington, D.C. James had studied medicine at Howard University. Isabella was a graduate of Oberlin College. They were of a generation shaped by the high hopes for racial concord that followed the American Civil War. But these hopes had faded by 1889, the year of the congregation's founding, and America had largely given in to racism. Still, members of this new congregation, mixed in race from the beginning, held on to the ideal of friendship across lines that might otherwise divide. Capitulation to racism couldn't happen *inside* the church of Christ.

The Howards found this confidence galvanizing, like some defiant candle holding its flame against the wind. By that time, however, the larger institution of Adventism was itself wavering. Toward the end of 1889, an article in the *Review and Herald* actually defended the separation of the races at a camp meeting in the South. And at just this point, Dr. Howard raised a voice of protest. He went straight to the church's president to make the case that "the more nationalities we can have in the church, the more like the future state the church will be." This, he explained, would be "strong evidence" in favor of the gospel message.

Some ten years later, one observer said this pioneering congregation was still a "living miracle," its harmony a "great surprise" to the world around it. But now the Adventist bureaucracy was cowering even more before the unholy fashions of the day, and pressure to break the church in two, one congregation Black and the other White, was mounting.

Again Dr. Howard spoke out, this time in a letter to Ellen White. "One of the strongest points of the Adventist cause in Washington," he said, was the reality of Blacks and Whites worshiping together.

Two years later, Ellen White stood before the congregation herself and saw what was increasingly rare at that time in America: Blacks and Whites singing and praying together. She preached that day from John 17, where Jesus, facing death, prays to the Father for His followers. They don't " 'belong to the world,' " He says, but He has " 'sent them into the world.' " Then He asks that " 'they may all be one . . . so that the world may believe that you have sent me.' "[13]

An inventor's *claims* may fall flat, but you can't refute a better mousetrap. In the same way, Christian words may fall flat, but it's hard to refute better lives, hard to dismiss communities that seem like living miracles. That's what Ellen White knew the day she preached her sermon on Jesus' famous prayer. That's what Dr. Howard understood when he twice dug in his heels against the pull of compromise. And that's what explains the early church's success against the overwhelming dominance of paganism.

Churches—and the lives of the people inside them—are living laboratories. Over time, evidence accrues from these living laboratories, and the evidence counts for or against the core hypotheses, or core teachings, of the Christian faith.[14] The words ring true, in other words, only if the lives ring true. Ben Franklin's famous aphorism seems to apply perfectly: "Well done is better than well said."[15]

The aphorism applies, that is, unless you forget to say anything at all. The Christian mission requires the Christian message. And as we have seen in this chapter, nothing refutes your right, and even your obligation, to make the case that needs to be made. The gospel story needs to be told and told well.

But make no mistake about it: the key to the telling is the living.

---

1. Matthew 28:19, 20.
2. Concerning Peter, see Acts 10. Acts 13 records the beginning of Paul's first mis-

sionary journey, including his use (see verse 47) of Isaiah 49:6.

3. Here I rely on sociologist Rodney Stark, in *The Rise of Christianity* (Princeton, N.J.: Princeton University Press, 1996), chapters 1–3.

4. See ibid., chapter 4; for the quotes from Dionysius and Julian, see pages 82, 84, and 88; for the contrast between Christian and pagan virtues, *See also* pages 211, 212.

5. Ibid., chapters 5 and 7. Stark uses the phrase "revitalization movement" on, e.g., 78 and 161. For the remark on pagan contempt for human flesh, I rely on David Bentley Hart, *The Beauty of the Infinite* (Grand Rapids, Mich.: Eerdmans, 2003), 106, 107.

6. Romans 10:14, 15; I quote more of Isaiah 52:7 than Paul does in Romans 10.

7. On peace, see, e.g., Psalm 34:14; Matthew 5:9; and Ezekiel 34:25–31. Adventist theologian Gottfried Oosterwal writes that the "church's mission" is to "participate in God's own mission," in *Mission: Possible* (Nashville: Southern Publishing Association, 1972), 69.

8. I rely on James Carroll, *Constantine's Sword: The Church and the Jews* (Boston: Houghton Mifflin Company, 2001), 185, 211; also, for quotes from Urban II, on David Chidester, *Christianity: A Global History* (San Francisco: HarperSanFrancisco, 2000), 177; and Justo L. González, *The Story of Christianity*, vol. 1 (San Francisco: Harper and Row, 1984), 292.

9. Lyrics to both songs widely available on the Internet. I thank Jeremy Scriven for this reference.

10. Abraham Joshua Heschel, *Moral Grandeur and Spiritual Audacity*, ed. Susannah Heschel (New York: Noonday, 1997), xxii. Quoted in James Carroll, *Constantine's Sword* (New York: Houghton Mifflin, 2001), 48.

11. Concerning Caesar, see, e.g., Brian J. Walsh and Sylvia C. Keesmaat, *Colossians Remixed: Subverting the Empire* (Downers Grove, Ill.: InterVarsity Press, 2004) 89, 90. The quotes, in order, are from Colossians 1:15, 2:8, 9. (Some argue, of course, that this letter comes from a disciple of Paul.)

12. See Colossians 3:15; also Luke 1:76–79.

13. Douglas Morgan told this story on November 21, 2008, at the annual meeting of the Adventist Society for Religious Studies. His research will be published in a forthcoming history of this congregation. The "observer" was Albion F. Ballenger. The phrases quoted from the Bible are from John 17:14, 18, 21, and 23.

14. For an argument to this effect, see Nancey Murphy, *Theology in the Age of Scientific Reasoning* (Ithaca, N.Y.: Cornell University Press, 1993), 196.

15. See, e.g., "The Quotations Page," http://www.quotationspage.com/quotes/Benjamin_Franklin/21. Accessed December 1, 2008.

12

Making a Difference

Ollie Petruzel lived just outside of Washington, D.C., where teenagers had credit cards and some drove BMWs to class. Friday nights he and his friends would gather at the McDonald's restaurant on Rolling Road, looking for a party.

He was one of the lucky ones of the world. He and his friends had more than enough of money and cars, and what's more, they had time to hang out together. But when a newspaper reporter asked how Ollie felt about where he was, he said, "This is the most boring place I ever lived."

Perhaps his answer was partly a teenager's pose. But Ollie Petruzel did understand that when you have everything, that doesn't mean you're OK. Without a purpose that goes beyond consumption and carousing, you're trapped inside your own ego. Nothing sets your heart on fire. Nothing is vivid except what you lack—a sense of significance and passion and adventure.

From the start, this book has addressed familiar needs and longings: how we each want to be fully alive and to live our best and deepest dreams; how human hopes meet up with obstacles; how we live, all of us, in the space *between our dreams and disappointments*. And inside that space, one thing is sure: except for zombies and couch potatoes, nobody wants boring.

When another young man, known now as Alexander the Great, was about Ollie Petruzel's age, his father, a Greek king, gave him command of the left wing of the Macedonian cavalry. He was just eighteen when he put in the brilliant performance that established his genius and determined his lifework. The forces he led crushed the combined armies of Thebes and Athens. The battle made him seem unstoppable, and he went on to establish a ferocious empire. He swept east and styled himself the "Lord of Asia." He descended into Egypt and became both Pharaoh and "Son of God." But in the end, his soldiers grew tired and bitter and began to resist his desire to be worshiped as a living deity. During his troubled final year, his best friend died, and in the midst of grief and anger, he arranged for the man's attending physician to be . . . crucified.

Alexander died when he was thirty-two. He had lived a life of significance, passion, and adventure. In those days, writers in practically every culture considered a successful warrior to be the greatest of human figures—the very archetype of heroism. Alexander's accomplishments were unrivaled, and the ancients, who overlooked casualties and cruelty, called him "the Great," the man more to be admired than any other.[1]

From the day Abraham heard God's call to leave home and become a "blessing" for others, he and his descendants, or the best of them, stood apart. Far from bored, they had a compelling purpose and lived passionate lives. They weren't dream busters—not when they were at their best. Unlike the marauding Alexander, they were enhancers of dreams. From inside the covenant of peace, they took universal blessing, or the well-being of all, to be the grand and inviolate ideal. They wanted a world in which everyone could flourish.

All too often, Abraham's ideals have been dishonored—you will see this even in Scripture itself. But they are still ideals, and today these ideals seem far more convincing than those of Alexander. Tyranny, greed, and violence still infect human hearts and still blight the streets where people live. But today's poets and historians would hardly bestow an honorific like "the Great" upon a man of Alexander's staggering arrogance and cruelty. They would no more do this than do so for Hitler. It no longer seems that you have to be a warlord—or exploit and demean your neighbors in other ways—to find significance, passion, and adventure in life.

Your Mission, Your Calling

"The place God calls you to be is the place where your deep gladness and the world's deep hunger meet."[2] To anyone familiar with the biblical vision, these words from Frederick Buechner shine like crystal, for according to the testimony of Abraham's descendants, God does want you to find your deep gladness. And according to that same testimony, God does want you to notice the world's deep hunger and to do your best to relieve it.

In the heritage of Abraham, a life mission is a calling. It's not something you determine yourself, or only yourself. The Maker of the stars and seas *expects* you to take up a certain kind of mission and *inquires* about the progress you are making.

The adversaries of a prominent Russian rabbi denounced him to the government, and he was imprisoned in St. Petersburg. As he was awaiting trial, the chief warden came by his cell. When the warden noticed the rabbi's majestic face and that he was lost in meditation, he realized that the prisoner was a man of true substance. The warden, himself a thoughtful person, decided to pose some questions about the Bible. Eventually, he asked, "How are we to understand that God, who is all-knowing, asked Adam, 'Where are you?'" He wondered why an all-knowing God would have to ask.

The rabbi replied with a question of his own: "Do you believe the Bible is eternal, addressing everyone in every era?"

The warden said Yes.

"Well, then," the rabbi continued, "in every era God says to every person, 'Where are you—where are you on your life journey? How far have you come?'"

The rabbi was telling the warden that the best way to read the story from Genesis is to think of yourself as Adam and of God as addressing this question to you. The story isn't about God's knowledge; it's about

God's concern.[3] In Scripture, then, God *addresses* us—lays claim to our attention, inquires about our lives, calls us to action.

According to the Gospels, God's address now comes to humanity through Jesus. In Mark, Jesus' first words to His disciples are "Follow me." In John, His last words are "Follow me."[4] So when you consider your life mission as a Christian, the one thing that matters most is following Jesus, being a disciple. God calls you away from the prison of self and frees you for radical forgiveness and passionate generosity. And if Jesus is at once the face of God and the face of ideal humanity, then you respond to the divine call precisely by throwing yourself, as He did, into the furrow of human need.[5] You do all you can, as He did, for your brother and your sister.

In one of Jesus' best-known parables, all this becomes vivid and unmistakable, like a trumpet blast piercing the silence. All people stand before the "Son of man" to hear a judgment upon their lives. And the one question that matters, they learn, is the question of compassion: have you shown compassion to others? For whatever you have done to one of the "least of these who are members of my family," the Son of man declares, you have done "to me."[6]

The Son of man is Jesus. The message is that Jesus so identifies with human feeling as to think of every face as if it were His own. You see *His* eyes in the face of every person, especially the neediest and most vulnerable of all. This makes every face in some sense holy. Every one. Without exception.

The poet and memoirist Kathleen Norris writes about imagining herself in a conversation with an elderly man. Suddenly, the man's face becomes "impossibly beautiful." She continues: "I can't escape the feeling that at this moment, in this unlikely setting, *I am looking into the face of Christ. And Christ is looking back at me.*"[7]

Nothing conveys human need as does a face. And as soon as you think of a particular face as if it were Christ's own, the impact sharpens. Such a face you cannot ignore.

The winter my father's health suddenly declined, my two brothers and I took turns going to Spokane to be with him in the hospital and to drive our mother there and then home at night. We all knew Dad might never again swing a golf club or drive a car. His face told us that he knew too.

While we sat with him, nurses and other professionals came into the room. They were strangers to my father, yet they offered him their tender mercies. I was moved. Later, I told my daughter, Christina, how I felt. A nurse herself, she was working in Baltimore, and I wanted her to talk about the kind of person you have to be in order to care for patients the way those strangers were caring for my dad.

Christina simply told me a story. One day she entered a hospital room and found that the bed was empty. Her eighty-year-old patient had shuffled with all his gear into the bathroom. Before she got to him, he sensed her presence and called out to her. His voice was anxious. He had finished—and was stuck. "I hate to ask you," he said. "I hate to ask you . . . but I can't . . ." And Christina understood—she could see that her patient was too stiff to be able to clean himself.

I knew what happened next. I admired my daughter for it. And I saw in a newly heartfelt way that inside a hospital, compassion—extravagant, unstinting compassion—is the key. For caregivers to be as attentive to patients as they need to be, that kind of compassion has to be common-place. It has to be practically routine.

When you think about it, all this is amazing. Hospitals centered on the needs of ordinary people didn't even exist before Christ, and no one thought to pay much attention to the old and sick. So as I thought about my father and my daughter, I realized again the difference that God's call has made. The sense that every human face is holy really did take hold, and today, hospital care and people generous enough to offer it are available in most of the world.

But not everywhere, and not for everyone who needs the care. The me-first-I-can't-be-bothered frame of mind, widespread among the ancients, is all too common still. In a poem called "Faces," Maya Angelou makes the point. When you consider the title in gospel light, that alone brings you up short. Then the poem's last lines seize your attention like the screech of tires. The author is imagining someone with an upheld sign crying out for the wretched of the city. The scene both moves and disturbs her: "A poet screams 'CHRIST WAITS AT THE SUBWAY!' / But who sees?"

We are called to see—called to see and then to act.

So the gospel says. And, as Jesus knew, the call is a gift. If you "satisfy the needs of the afflicted," His Bible said, "then your light shall rise in the darkness and your gloom be like the noonday."[8] Jesus knew that the mission He calls us to is a release from the ego trap. There is deep gladness in it, and for the frail shell of our self-regard, it is the only invincible protection.

But how shall I respond to God's call when the world is so complicated? I have to make a living in a way that suits my aptitudes and circumstances. That is challenging enough. But because I cannot, by myself, relieve the world's deep hunger, or even my neighbor's, I need to enhance what I can do by interacting with the wider society. At church or city hall or elsewhere, I can try to influence people who have the capacity to help others flourish. I may even try to build a company or service organization myself. The journey is bound to feel a little bit like whitewater. How will I find my way?

If you make God's call your path to significance, passion, and adventure, it won't be enough just to be nice. Christ peers out from every human face, and the scale of obligation is too overwhelming. You *have* to consider how you will partner with a wider circle of people. You *have* to consider how you will make the most of surrounding institutions. You *have* to consider how you will relate to the powers that be.

As you know from you own heart, you won't find perfect helpers, not anywhere. You will run into the proverbial brick walls. And you will feel compromised just for cooperating with some people and institutions at all.

Dare to Be a Daniel

So, when you answer to God, how *do* you relate to the society around you?

Here, a story from the Hebrew Bible is particularly apt. I realized this anew the day I saw, in a Washington, D.C., gallery, the watercolor that now hangs in my office. It shows a man in a Washington subway station. He's wearing a ponytail—like an outsider, not a downtown lawyer—and he's standing beside a stopped train. Behind the train windows you can see people waiting in their seats for the exchange of passengers to finish. The man with the ponytail has a brush and some paint, and above the windows on the side of the train he is writing *Mene, mene tekel upharsin*.

The words the man is writing make up the famous "handwriting on the wall" from a story in the book of Daniel. Belshazzar, the Babylonian king, has made a "great festival" and is "drinking wine" and basking in the attention of a "thousand of his lords." Out of nowhere a human hand begins writing on the wall. Neither the king nor his wise men can read the message, and the king is terrified. He calls for Daniel, who has an uncanny aptitude for interpretation, and hears the awful truth.

Daniel explains that Belshazzar's grandfather, Nebuchadnezzar, "killed those he wanted to kill, kept alive those he wanted to keep alive, honored those he wanted to honor, and degraded those he wanted to degrade." Because of this, he was driven from the throne for a time. But Belshazzar has learned nothing from this, and the handwriting on the wall means that his kingdom's days are "numbered." He has been weighed on the scales—"weighed in the balances," as the King James Version puts it—and found wanting.[9]

Daniel speaks from inside the covenant of peace, where divine and human purposes coalesce around blessing for all.[10] The Babylonians have scorned this ideal, and Daniel bears a witness for God at the very nerve center of the culture where he lives.

He is close to that nerve center because he prepared for government service and eventually became a top administrator. For the question of life mission, or life calling, his story is a signal that God smiles upon engagement with the society you live in. It's a signal, too, that God embraces varied occupations, including ones you might not think of as particularly "religious." For life mission, the issue is not whether you work as a pastor or professor, artist or engineer, grocer or mechanic. Your aptitudes and opportunities do matter; you have to consider them. But most fundamentally, the question of life mission is about whether you stay true to God's covenant of peace and actually contribute to human flourishing, actually honor the sanctity of every human face.

Adventists revere the book of Daniel for its apocalyptic imagination as well as for the courage of Daniel himself. Weird, poetic images flare off its pages like fireworks, telling the truth of human greed and horror even as they draw you into God-intoxicated hope. The book promises a new world. At the same time, it invites you into engaged participation in the world today. But not copycat participation. As an apocalyptic masterpiece, the book of Daniel yanks you away from mindless convention, away from obeisance to whatever happens to be the case or whoever happens to be in power.

All this, too, matters for how you think about life mission.

The book's beginning tells a tale of defeat and deportation. Nebuchadnezzar besieges Jerusalem. He walks off with its treasures. He marches its best young men into servitude and exile.

He wants to reeducate these young men into usefulness, and he commissions teachers to train them in "the literature and language" of Babylon.[11] At the beginning of chapter 3, we saw that the self you show the world takes its shape from the stories you dwell on and the characters you identify with. Nebuchadnezzar understands this, and he tries to instill in these young minds a new story—a story alien to them and helpful to him. What better way to make them compliant functionaries?

As for Daniel and his closest friends, they resist. They do excel physically, as the king wishes. They do shine in literature and wisdom. They do end up with positions in the king's court. But they say No when they have to. They refuse to be brainwashed. They remember who they are.

Daniel continues to distinguish himself. For one thing, he has a God-given knack for dreams, or the gift, in other words, of apocalyptic imagination. And when Nebuchadnezzar needs help in remembering and interpreting a worrisome dream, Daniel comes in with a riveting report. The king saw, he declares, a great statue with a head of gold, chest and arms of silver, middle and thighs of bronze, legs of iron, and feet partly of iron and partly of clay. Then he saw a stone striking the statue's feet, and the whole thing crashing down and breaking into pieces as light as chaff. The wind carried the pieces away as if they were nothing, and the stone "became a great mountain and filled the whole earth."

What does the dream mean? Daniel dares to say. The statue's main body parts, made of different metals, stand for kingdoms—the head of gold for Nebuchadnezzar's, and the rest, for kingdoms that will follow his. All these human kingdoms, Daniel continues, will pass away. Every king is vulnerable—each one a sign, as we might now say, that today's peacock is tomorrow's feather duster. Finally, however, the "God of heaven will set up a kingdom that shall never be destroyed."[12] One day the divine kingdom will nullify all grandiose and heartless ones—and deep transformation, true healing of the world, will take place.

Daniel's performance is as gutsy as any prophet's. So it's surprising when Nebuchadnezzar falls to the ground as a gesture of respect for him. He even rewards him with a better position. But Nebuchadnezzar takes the dream and its interpretation to be a windfall of political intelligence—information he can use to his own imperial ends. Now he can set out to defy the prospect Daniel has laid out. Starting immediately, he can fend off threats to his hegemony.

Soon the king has built a massive "golden statue"—all gold, all Babylon—and is *demanding* that everyone fall down and worship it. Here three of Daniel's friends take center stage. They refuse to join the heedless masses bending their knees to this symbol of arrogance and power. For their defiance, Nebuchadnezzar throws them into a "furnace of blazing fire." Miraculously, they escape.[13]

By now a theme is evident, and it casts a crucial light on the question of life mission or life calling: *As God's child in a world that pushes God away, you do participate in the life and culture around you. You do say Yes when you can. But as God's child, you say No when the world asks you to sell out. You say No because the world never has the last word. Not the last word about human values. Not the last word about the human prospect. Only God has the last word.*

Daniel keeps interacting with his society—sometimes to assist the powers that be, and sometimes, like the man in the watercolor, to resist them. Once, having angered Darius the Mede, he spends the night in a den of lions. So Daniel knows difficulty, and he feels, now and then, the bleakness that steals into any human heart. But like Habakkuk, he somehow hears words that renew his faith in the faithfulness of God, and his courage and passion return.[14] Apocalyptic visions continue to billow out of his imagination, putting arrogance and evil in bold relief, yet always moving on to hope.

An old kids' song goes: "Dare to be a Daniel / Dare to stand alone. / Dare to have a purpose firm, / Dare to make it known." When you take the dare, you become a purveyor of hope—a foe of arrogance, a friend of compassion and peace. All the while, you keep enough distance from whatever happens to be the case or whoever happens to be in power to assure that you aren't in league with the old world but in league with the new. Only then does your life mission rise above the ordinary. Only then do you make the kind of difference that renews the human spirit—that addresses people's needs and even changes hearts and minds.

Keeping Your Focus

Daniel lived with depravity around him and hope in his heart. It was a great hope, luminous with visions of God's coming victory over evil. And one thing it teaches is that just when your hope for a new world is most intense, you *engage* the present world. Just then you busy yourself, the best way you can, with the healing of the here-and-now.

Daniel was immersed in apocalyptic fervor, and his hope kept him from turning into a compliant functionary. Still, he threw himself—but not unreservedly—into government service. That was how, in the spirit of Jeremiah, he sought "the peace of the city" where he was living.[15] That was how, under trying circumstances, he tried to be the blessing God wanted him to be.

Jesus was likewise immersed in apocalyptic fervor. In His prayer for the disciples, He told the Father that they "do not belong to the world." Yet He also said that He was sending them "into the world."[16] The prayer seems like an echo of Daniel's life.

In the story that defines Christian existence, Jesus, of course, is the One who best reveals God's true colors to humanity. So, for the question of how to engage the world around you, He provides the final benchmark.

Jesus' own life was a response to the covenant of peace first intimated in the call of Abraham. He knew that the covenant is an expression of God's love and grace. He knew that it asks for a response from each of us. And He also knew that the right response is the life mission of every disciple. When He spoke a blessing upon those who embrace that mission, He said they were peacemakers: "Blessed are the peacemakers, for they will be called children of God."[17] Then, with His whole life story, He showed that the basic fiber of the peacemaking mission is radical forgiveness, a love so irrepressible that it reaches out even to the enemy.

I need not fill this out by circling back to all I have said before. But I do want to offer one last summary of Adventist conviction. You remember from chapter 2 that delegates to the 1861 organizing meeting for a "conference" of Adventist congregations in Michigan made a simple pledge to one another. Based on further developments through the early decades, the pledge seemed incomplete, and in chapter 4, I offered a refinement. But in light of the long scriptural reflection we are just completing, it seems best to bring in the theme Jesus put at the *very heart* of the disciples' calling. I suggest now that the best and simplest pledge Adventists could make to one another is this: *Thanks to the gift of grace, and for the purpose of blessing all, we take up the peacemaking mission and join together in keeping the commandments of God and the faith of Jesus.*

Any pledge of Christian loyalty takes you aback when you think about it. The standard is so high. But if a high standard is how you find your deep gladness, the high standard is worth reaching for. And if the basis of your pledge is grace, you can aim high in the confidence that God won't shunt you aside when you miss the mark. God forgives, and God restores.

How can you keep your focus?

We saw in chapter 3 that Jesus made a habit of Sabbath keeping, and here is a vital clue.[18] On the Sabbath you suspend your ordinary busyness, and, in the company of others, refresh your connection with grace.

You feel anew the forgiveness and empowering presence of the God who comes to earth in Christ.

Jesus Himself did these things. He rested from routine in order to celebrate the wonder of God's faithfulness and love. He read Scripture in the company of others, putting aside the "language and literature" of the wider world so He could savor again His own story.

The Sabbath heightens consciousness. Distractions subside. Forgetfulness is ruptured. Now you realize in a full-blooded way that everything you have is a gift. Now the promise of peace is somehow renewed. Now, in the "recitation of your gratitude to God," you gain strength for the days to come.[19]

It's human to dream dreams. It's divine to help make the best of those dreams come true. That is what God does, and that is the Good News that underlies all Christian faith. Of course, you are God's partner along the way, and the work is hard. Sometimes it is harrowing. But if, like Jesus, you pay disciplined attention to God and to God's story, you build muscle. Through worship and reading, conversation and prayer, you stay connected, and from the connection you gain energy and fortitude.

God's mission takes you on a path from common places to uncommon ones. Here you live by the promise of peace and become a peacemaker yourself. Here you enjoy the company of the likeminded and work together for the blessing of all. Here you step away from the world, yet engage it so creatively that you become the vanguard of a new humanity.

In all this is the deep gladness that meets the world's deep hunger, and it is the place you are called to be.

---

1. Ollie Petruzel's comment appeared in a Washington *Post* feature story around 1990. For the account of Alexander, I have relied on Thomas Cahill, *Desire of the Everlasting Hills: The World Before and After Jesus* (New York: Nan A. Talese / Anchor Books, 1999), 15–24.

2. Frederick Buechner, *Beyond Words: Daily Readings in the ABCs of Faith* (San Francisco: HarperSanFrancisco, 2004), 405. I thank Rebekah Wang, my wife, for bringing this sentence to my attention.

3. Martin Buber tells this story in *The Way of Man: According to the Teachings of the Hasidism* (New York: Lyle Stuart, 1995), 9, 10. The Bible story is in Genesis 3.

4. Mark 1:17; John 21:22.

5. I love the metaphor of the "furrow," which I borrow from Ellen White, in *The Desire of Ages,* 622. It is an echo of the wheat-seed parable in John 12:24.

6. See Matthew 25:31–40.

7. Kathleen Norris, *Amazing Grace: A Vocabulary of Faith* (New York: Riverhead Books, 1998), 285. My italics.

8. Isaiah 58:10.

9. Daniel 5 records the story. Key quoted phrases are from verses 1, 9, 25–27.

10. In 10:18, 19, a troubled Daniel hears someone "in human form" (NRSV) wish him "peace" (KJV).

11. Daniel 1:4. The "Chaldeans" mentioned in this verse were the people who ruled over Babylon.

12. See Daniel 2; the quoted phrases are from verses 35 and 44.

13. Daniel 3. The quoted phrase appears in both verses 15 and 17.

14. See chapter 10, not least verses 18, 19, where one "in human form" says, " 'Do not fear, greatly beloved, you are safe. Be strong and courageous!' "

15. The phrase is from Jeremiah 29:7. I quote, as in chapter 5, from the King James Version; "welfare" is how, in this verse, the NRSV translates *shalom.*

16. See John 17:14–18.

17. Matthew 5:9.

18. See Luke 4:16.

19. Michael Fishbane, *Sacred Attunement* (Chicago: University of Chicago Press, 2008), 123.

General Index

Page numbers refer either to quotes or important allusions in the text proper; the letter *n* indicates an endnote.

Aristotle, 79

atheists, atheism, 89–91

atonement, 98–109. *See also* reconciliation; salvation. *See also under* Christ; Jesus

authorities, 107, 142, 143; Daniel and the, 152–155; Jewish and Roman, 39, 41, 78

autonomy, 115

Autumn Council of 1921, 28

Babylon, Babylonians, 38, 87, 92, 152

"Bad, Bad Leroy Brown," 11, 19n1

Ballenger, Albion F., 145n13

baptism, 44, 114, 120

Barnes, Michael, 133n12

Barth, Karl, 16, 19n3

Bartimaeus, 51–53, 55

Bates, Joseph, 23, 25

Battle Creek: Adventist mayor of, 26; College, 26, 27; Sanitarium, 26

Beatitudes, 40, 58, 64

beloved community, 13, 111–122, 142. *See also* church

Belshazzar, 152

Bible: as addressing personal journeys, 148; Christ as key to interpretation of, 118; as
   master story, 31, 32, 44;

blessing, 25, 35, 37, 38, 40, 41, 45, 59, 78, 80, 100, 108, 131, 147, 152

Blind Boys of Alabama, 82

Block, Gay, 33n13, 71n25

border-crossing, 127, 129, 131, 132

Bosnia, 20, 68, 69

Bridges, Ruby, 72, 73, 82

Britton, Mary, 66

Buber, Martin, 158n3

Buechner, Frederick, 148

Bull, Malcolm, 33n15

Butler, Jonathan M., 33n9, 56n5

Byington, Anson, 33n7

Caesar, 59, 78, 142, 145n11

Cahill, Thomas, 45n3, 45n12, 157n1

Camacho, Manuel, 66

Campolo, Tony, 135

Camus, Albert, 89, 90, 96n4

Scripture Index

Page numbers refer either to quotes or important allusions in the text proper; the letter *n* indicates an endnote.

Scripture Index

If you have been blessed by the insights in this book, you'll want to read these also.

Searching for a God to Love (Updated edition)
Chris Blake

Control issues. Unloving, judgmental people. Boredom.
It had little to do with God, but it all got mixed up together.

You have questions.
You have doubts.
You've been hurt.

You ache for something more than rhetoric, preaching,
and simplistic reasoning.

Great.
You qualify to take the journey this book defines.

Paperback. 256 pages.
ISBN 10: 0-8163-2304-6

Everlasting Gospel, Ever-changing World
Introducing Jesus to a Skeptical Generation
Jon Paulien

The gospel never changes; should our methods?

God's Word is eternal, but times change. Proof texts mean nothing to today's skeptics. Fortunately, God provides innovative methods of outreach. Jon Paulien offers his insights into the mission of the church and the opportunity we have to witness in new ways to new people. To bring people to Christ, we need more than correct doctrine. We need a living relationship with Jesus, reflected daily in faith, hope, and love.

Paperback. 190 pages.
ISBN 10: 0-8163-2262-7